HOUSEHOLD ECOLOGY

HOUSEHOLD ECOLOGY

JULIA PERCIVALL AND PIXIE BURGER

PRENTICE-HALL, INC., *Englewood Cliffs, N. J.*

Household Ecology
by Julia Percivall and Pixie Burger
Copyright © 1971 by Julia Edith Percivall and Rosaylmer Burger
All rights reserved. No part of this book may be
reproduced in any form or by any means, except for
the inclusion of brief quotations in a review, without
permission in writing from the publisher.
ISBN: 0-13-395889-2
Library of Congress Catalog Card Number: 77-168492
Printed in the United States of America T
Prentice-Hall International, Inc., London
Prentice-Hall of Australia, Pty. Ltd., Sydney
Prentice-Hall of Canada, Ltd., Toronto
Prentice-Hall of India Private Ltd., New Delhi
Prentice-Hall of Japan, Inc., Tokyo

This book is
dedicated to everyone,
for we are all on
this earth together.

CONTENTS

HOUSEHOLD ECOLOGY

NOTE

Although this book is written in the first person singular, it is actually the product of equal collaboration between two writers. The first person singular format is chosen for two reasons:

1. It is easier to read.
2. It was infinitely easier to write!

Above all, it is far less clumsy than continually saying "we," which would probably cause grammar to obscure the subject at hand.

Julia Percivall and Pixie Burger

INTRODUCTION

A NEW CONCEPT

Ecology is a currently popular word for a science which, in the practical sense, has been with us since the beginning of mankind. But until a short time ago, many of us did not know of the word's existence. It was not the sort of thing we learned at our mother's knee, mostly because mother didn't know about it either.

Today's mothers *do* know—and the new generations should learn its meaning at an early age. The fact that change is constant underscores the hope and future of mankind, now faced with what is frequently referred to *in toto* as the "ecological problem." Basically, ecology is that branch of biology which deals with the relations between organisms and their environment; it is also the branch of sociology concerned with the spacing of people and of institutions, and their resulting interdependency (*The American College Dictionary*).

In other words, the right balance between creation and destruction creates a cycle: this chain of building up and breaking down forms the wheel of nature and of life. Man is a part of this continual chain of activity.

The point has now been reached, however, where man must implement a whole new concept of life (and of the art of living) if that cycle is to continue—which, so far as we are concerned, means if we are to continue enjoying life on this earth.

In the months since pollution became a household word, the average reader has been overwhelmed with facts and figures and reports and opinions. Groggily, one rises to one's feet to ask if the situation is *really* serious. The answer is yes. Very.

The next question, of course, is: Is it hopeless? Are we truly destined to disappear off the face of the earth before the turn of the next century, as has been suggested? Fortunately, no. We have time and opportunity to take steps to prevent this from happening.

This leads us naturally to inquire: How much time, and exactly what steps?

Scientific statistics make the situation quite clear: *we have thirty years in which to clean up the world.*

That time starts *now,* and it is a grace period for positive action. We must not only clean up the mess mankind has already made (in many cases unwittingly), but also set our life styles along better, sounder, healthier, and more ecologically balanced paths.

To be sure the scientists, the industrialists, the "big wheels" of this world must do their share—but cleaning up the world's pollution is not exclusively their duty. We are all in this together, each one of us, because even in death—but especially in life—we are part of the ecological chain. There's no opting out.

Quite literally, ecology begins with the individual at home. If you think of a house or apartment as an organism within the total environment, you can immediately see the importance of its relationship to its surroundings. Is its refuse output more than the immediate environment can absorb (refuse includes smoke into the surrounding air, sewage into the sewage system, as well as the trash overflow in the form of discarded household objects and organic "garbage")? How does the home as an organism affect other living organisms in the vicinity (plants, wildlife, *and* men)? Ecological disasters have a way of happening on a very small but painful scale, even in the midst of cities.

Take the case of a tenement neglected by a landlord. Filth invades it, rats inhabit it. So much for Step One. Step Two: Rats carry disease which infects the tenants . . .

The repercussions of neglect, abuse, or mismanagement are fast and usually fatal. We are only beginning to realize the truth in the old saying, "you reap what you sow." The very personal dangers of having "sown" pollution far and wide hardly need to be underlined for the thinking man and woman.

There are thousands of steps to be taken in rebalancing the health of the world. Some are gigantic, the kind to be taken by powerful industrial giants, while others, though small and individual, desperately need to be taken by each one of us, en masse.

Starting in the late sixties, and snowballing as we entered the

1970's, the figures and lists and hints began to bombard us on all sides. We have learned, for example, such widely different facts as:

1. Filter-tip cigarette butts should never be thrown into toilets or any drains that lead to either cesspools or sewage systems. Extremely difficult to break down and process, the filters clog up the works badly and are harmful to cesspools and detrimental to even the largest of city sewage-processing plants.

2. Dyestuffs that do not break down biologically are to be regarded with a wary eye. Apart from certain kinds of food coloring, brightly colored facial tissues have also come under scrutiny.

3. To help diminish the mountain of refuse that presently threatens to engulf us, carrying a canvas shopping bag is an excellent idea. That way at least some of the multi-layers of paper can be avoided on any shopping expedition. At the very least, one can help slow down the accumulation of discarded paper by using paper shopping bags many times over.

4. New products, extolled as "clean" or "nonpolluting" or "ecologically sound," are certainly worth taking a look at. Some of them may be more advertising claim than actual value, but the comment they cause and the enthusiasm they engender shows the mood of the buyer market.

5. All those wire coat hangers that accumulate with every trip to the cleaners' should be neatly tied together and handed *back* to the cleaners'—rather than get thrown out with the garbage. Hangers are bulky and awkward and add vastly to the garbage problem. The cleaner can recycle them. And if he won't take them back, find a dry cleaner who will.

6. Those who like writing letters are being urged on all sides to do their bit. See something you find ecologically unsound? Write a letter to the outfit perpetrating the bad deed, with copies sent off to any agency you think should be aware of the problem. And yes, letters *do* have an effect on business, industry, public officials, committees.

7. Clubs and other groups dedicated to the ecological cleanup of the world have been formed, and are still forming all over the country. Joining one adds your strength to the world cleanup

movement, and since there are many different branches of endeavor within the whole movement, chances are that almost everybody can find a club of specific interest.

Inescapably, our attitudes and outlook contribute to the general picture. Popular concepts presently under fire include the idea that air and water are free commodities. Within the context of the new approach, the "gift" of life carries with it certain innate obligations to permit the rest of life to go on living, too. Air and water are free only if we see to it that they are equally free—not only of charge, but also of pollution—for everyone else.

For a great many years the idea of continuous economic growth was the generally accepted answer to all the world's ills. An ever-increasing Gross National Product, said the believers, would eventually put two chickens in every pot, all over the world. All we had to do was make bigger and better and more and more . . . But, as enthusiasts are apt to do when their ideas blaze, the enthusiastic theorists forgot one factor. The world we live on is not an ever-expanding entity. Its natural resources, though vast, are eventually finite.

The chain of life replenishes many of the sources we use—soil, for example, to which all "used" life (organic matter that has decomposed) returns to make more soil. But if we totally ruin something, or destroy a species, or exhaust any of our natural resources, there is no friendly neighborhood planet we can run to to borrow some more.

Much of the harm that man has done in the past he did without realizing what he was doing. But much of the harm being done right now is being perpetrated by individuals who either do not think in ecological terms at all, or whose attitude is, "What the heck, it won't hit for another couple of generations, so why should I worry now?"

These feckless souls are in error—our thirty years' grace have already begun: the harm is with us now.

Most of those who read this book can hope to be around thirty years from now. Half the present population of the world was born after World War II. And the world is not going to go on in an unchanging state for 29½ years and then suddenly burn out. The damage is already showing up, and the ecological warning signs will get more insistent and more uncomfortable *for all of us* with each passing year. It is not even a question of "cleaning up the world for the sake of our children." The discomforts and disasters are going to hit *us,* as well as them.

They do not *have* to, however. The frightening statistical projections are true—but they are still *projections.* It is certainly well within our human capabilities to change habits, mores, modes, and fashions so that the projections do not become realities. If we change the present conditions, we change the future, too. Both are goals we must set for ourselves.

It will take more than an "Earth Day" to do it, although no doubt 1970's Earth Day did much to awaken the public to the facts. It will take more than slogans ("If you're not part of the solution—you're part of the pollution"), though these too play their part in alerting people to the dangers of the situation.

Above all, we must realize and thoroughly understand that the movement toward a more sound ecology is *not* a fad that will pass into oblivion when the next fashion captures the public's fancy. The environment is a fact of life, and those who think its popularity will pass away into oblivion should consider the other things that must, perforce, be obliterated with it—the joy of living, if not of life itself. Of course there are the opportunists (and some are cited in subsequent chapters) who will try to manipulate the issues to promote their own desires. But none of this is going to alter the environmental issues themselves, because, even if men can be manipulated by words and ideas (and this is not always true) nature doesn't care what they say on television.

The issues can and must be dealt with at all levels: governmental, industrial, community, individual. We've all seen, heard, read about, or experienced the annoyances of pollution at this stage: eye-stinging smoggy air, foaming tap water, food that tastes of cardboard (and worse), cosmetics that blotch the skin, potions that pollute rather than cure, the empty promises, the downright lies. All these and many other ills have come at us thicker and faster during the past several decades.

These were the decades once so proudly hailed as the years of the affluent society—the society of overconsumption in many areas. Affluence seems to have produced more physical, mental, and spiritual pollution than any other period in the history of mankind, and among the very few good things one can say about this era is that it is now over.

Not finished, mind you: the end of an era does not come overnight. But despite the pockets of ignorance and resistance to change, conspicuous consumption is being called by its real name these days: waste.

On the individual and household level (which is what this book is all about) there are two main things a person can do to effect change and help restore ecological balance.

1. You can protect yourself from presently polluted conditions.
2. You can see to it that your own cycle of goods and life is well-balanced, nonpolluting, and ecologically constructive.

In the protective sense, we can help combat the effects of pollution beyond our immediate sphere of control, upon all our lives. In the constructive sense, we can restock and refurnish whatever parts of the environment lie within our individual control—by natural means and with natural nutrients.

Whether he owns a home or rents an apartment, if each person's cycles are balanced and beneficial, then all of us benefit from each other's cycles in multiple form. Homes, garden, community, countryside—the circle of influence grows gradually wider and wider. Be it in planting a flower, or in the letter of protest against a belching factory stack, or in the refusal to buy an insecticide that is harmful to the songbirds, the ultimate power *does* lie in the hands of the individual.

Which is why, in the final analysis, we must all play a part in initiating change and restoring the ecological balance.

Part One

ECOLOGY IN THE MARKET PLACE

1. Ecological Shopping

The business of business is concerned with the constant increase of commerce and the proportionate exchange of money. Although life and commerce are not necessarily mutually exclusive, the ecologically aware consumer might understandably think that they were. Industrial pollution alone (factories belching smoke into the air, plants discharging poisonous waste into lakes and rivers) is enough to make most of us think that where big business goes after big profits, then ecology takes a back seat.

But it is necessary that we try to maintain a reasonable balance in our thinking, just as we fervently desire a balance in all things around us. Commerce should not be condemned as wholly bad: scratching-the-earth for a living is still more for chickens than people. Industry is part and parcel of twentieth-century life, like it or no.

But it should be up to industry and commerce to produce and sell objects and services that are necessary and/or enhancing to human life. Just as make-work projects are a waste of time, so are there objects sold that are pollutant both to the earth and to the fabric of human life. For example, I fail to see any worth in an electrical appliance costing twenty dollars that serves only one function: to boil an egg. This machine uses metal, burns up electricity, costs money in promotion, advertising, merchandising, etc.—and ends up doing something that can be done much cheaper in the age-old way.

There *are* areas in which ecology and commerce succeed in complementing each other: housing shelters us, clothing protects us, food nourishes. Our need for the basic commodities of life, and industry's production of them, ought to attain a certain balance.

However, closer examination often shows that balance to be

7

unfairly weighted on the side of commerce. It is as though some
man-made law (the law of Mammon, perhaps?) dictates that the
priorities should always swing toward the financial, rather than the
ecological, aspects of any given situation. It is time that this trend
was altered.

A good place to start this adjustment is right where you enter
the consumer buying-cycle. All stores and other merchandising
outlets sell on the basis of *caveat emptor*—"let the buyer
beware"—a chilly-sounding phrase if ever there was one. Let us
rephrase it to say, "let the buyer be informed"—and let him
receive his information unrestricted. *Correct* information, I hasten
to add, so that he or she truly knows the facts behind the item
offered for sale.

Whatever material items we buy will convert after varying
lengths of time into trash. Now the ecologically aware shopper has
two aims in mind.

1. To make the life span of the item between cash purchase
   and trash disposal as long and useful as possible (this does
   not apply to foodstuffs, naturally).
2. To discourage manufacturers from producing and marketing
   goods whose by-products or residues result in unnecessary
   amounts of trash—especially those kinds of garbage that
   cannot be broken down (and thus "recycled") by natural
   means.

After all the publicity that ecology has received, one would
think that industry would be only too eager to respond. Indeed it
is—but the question remains if the American marketplace has yet
to respond to ecology in any *meaningful* way.

A friend of mine was present at a top-echelon meeting at a large
public relations company, back when what the company calls the
"ecology bandwagon" began. The purpose of the meeting was how
to get onto that bandwagon. Environmental problems were briefly
mentioned, and then the meeting got down to the heart of the
matter: *How can we best make money out of this gimmick, both
for our clients and for ourselves?*

An attitude of "fatherly concern" and serious interest was what
was needed; campaigns were to be sketched out in accordance

with these guidelines. Only *image* and *attitude* counted: no serious concern for the environmental problems themselves was demonstrated at the meeting. After all, as one executive put it, "None of us is going to be here in fifty years' time, and meanwhile we have a business to run. . . ."

I think that this demonstrates quite clearly that ecological responsibility *must* begin with the consumer. Not only does it seem the natural starting point—it also seems the only place where it has a chance.

In the face of what some of the big guns are doing, however, what can one puny individual actually do? The answer is both surprising and encouraging: *plenty.* Never underestimate the power of the individual. Particularly when individual also means "consumer."

It is among the paradoxes of our time that, in an age of mass production, mass communication, and seemingly mass everything else, the individual can rise up on his own with greater ease and more prospect of success than ever before. A lone voice raised against common wrong is seldom alone for long. A responsible stand taken by one will soon be endorsed by others. It is our planet, our earth, our air and sea; merely by being born, we have a natural right to life. And where there is a right, there is also a corresponding responsibility.

The following pointers—some general, some specific—may serve as guidelines. They emphasize what most of us have known or suspected all along.

1. Do you really want the item in question? Do you really need it; moreover, can you really use it? An object purchased on a wrongly directed impulse can be as bad for the environment as it is for your budget. You find you don't need/want/use it, it clutters your living space for a while, and it is eventually discarded, thus adding to the garbage problem.

2. Whereas for some items, being disposable is an advantage (surgical dressings come to mind as one obvious example), there are items that, when used out of context, increase the garbage problem out of all proportion and, in some cases, lessen intangible qualities of life. Paper napkins, for instance, are fine

for a specific children's party or picnic, but for day-to-day use cloth napkins are cheaper in the long run and they do impart a touch of added civility to a meal. I realize that elegance is hard to bother with when coping with the milk, manners, and table mores of three children all under the age of 8, but one needs to start somewhere. As family members grow older and more responsible in their attitudes, it should be possible to cut down generally on the day-to-day disposables. After all, it's really not much harder to pick up cloth napkins and drop them in the washer than to pick up paper ones and drop them in the garbage can.

3. Must you continue to buy products that come swaddled in layers and layers of wrappings? Obviously some packaging is necessary, but the paper bag over the cardboard box over the paper wrap over the plastic wrap, sometimes even over the *inner* plastic wrap over the stiff plastic product cover, is super-fluous—not only a wasteful use of resources, but already proven to be an added burden to the environment.

   Sometimes the overpackaging syndrome produces other kinds of disadvantages, too. An example: the thin plastic wrapping on string beans, the kind of covering that keeps them firmly on their green pressed-paper supermarket tray, also encourages the growth of a fuzzy mold. If you are a hopeful bean-eater, both wrapping and mold are working against you. Another thing wrong with that sealed-in plastic vegetable business: it's a great way to conceal the rotten side of a tomato, the punched-in peach bottom, the punctured pepper. Boycott, protest, write an indignant letter, shop elsewhere. Yes, there are still places where the vegetables are not prepackaged with presealed mold spores. And there are going to be more, too, if only protest and demand for them increase.

4. Remember that big business is big because there are a great many consumers buying the products. But what happens when consumers decide to stop buying? Sometimes it takes a while for the word to spread and the sales to fall (look what happened to cranberries in the 1950's, and more recently, to tuna and swordfish), though often it happens all of a rush. But in the

long run, public disapproval (in other words, the voices of individual angry consumers) causes definitive change. Even the public relations men admit that they can preserve a company's image only just so long, by means of a carefully planned campaign. After a short while, no amount of whitewashing is going to obscure the truth. That time can be vastly shortened, however, by a thinking consumer who makes reasoned, selected purchases—followed up by protest and boycott, of course, should the purchases prove unsatisfactory.

5. Plastic is both hero and villain, depending on how, when, where, and how many times it is put to use. Since bacteria cannot decompose it, it causes difficulties in disposal and upon incineration, frequently producing harmful gases and a solid, sooty residue. It is simply not the all-purpose wonder manufacturers would have us believe. A case in point were the plastic lawn and leaf bags. The sales banner proclaimed their capacity (33 to 40 gallons), their convenience ("Rid your garden of unwanted leaves—NOW!"), their size (holds six bushels), and their advantages (no messy leftovers). They were being distributed by a large merchandising chain—and they just about epitomize the harm we can do when we are ignorant of the facts.

Leaves should be reincorporated into the earth. To pack them into plastic bags and cart them away to be burned—along with the plastic—is madness. Anyone continuing to burn leaves and plastic, thus burdening the air with known harmful components and simultaneously robbing the earth of potential leaf-mold nutrients, is acting in dismal ecological style. Ditto the buyer and burner of plastic bags.

When people *know* the hazards they are incurring, the chances are very high that they'll change their tactics. But the hazards have to be recognized first. Investigate what happens to waste after it leaves your household.

6. To buy items made from any part of an animal—be it fish, fowl, or mammal—that is in any way an endangered species is the height of shortsightedness. Once a species is extinct, of course, its own troubles are over; but that is when ours are likely to begin.

For example: the widespread slaughter of hippopotamuses in one section of Africa was hard on more than just the hippos. The scarcity of the breed quite naturally lowered the amount of hippo dung usually found in the area. A certain insect, whose food supply and life cycle depend on hippo-dung, therefore had its population slashed. These insects normally prey on a certain disease-carrying bug. Since the first kind of insect was diminished in numbers, the disease-carrying kind flourished wildly. And, as is their natural habit, they carried a dangerous tropical disease to the human beings in the neighborhood—only in far greater numbers than ever before, since there were now so many more of these disease-carriers around. Eventually, some of the very hunters who had been killing hippos (and to what purpose was that slaughter, one wonders?) suffered nature's revenge.

There is a certain element of black humor in this story, until one considers that innocent people also were afflicted by the uncontrollable spread of disease. And if exotic, this is far from being an isolated example. Any kind of willful destruction may well destroy a link in the ecological chain that will produce unforeseen, and sometimes disastrous, consequences. In the final analysis we should remember—*mankind* is an endangered species.

From the feminine angle, it is interesting to note that the world's wealthiest women either seldom wear furs, or wear only those which come from commercially raised animals. (I am not referring to women who marry wealthy men, but those who are wealthy in their own right.)

Queen Elizabeth II of England is one such woman: the ermine trim on a few of her ceremonial robes is the extent of her fur-wearing. Because of protocol, the English queen can lead only by example, not exhortation: privately, she is adamant against the senseless slaughter of animals for fashion.

Queen Juliana of the Netherlands is also vehement in her espousal of conservation and wildlife protection. Her young daughter, Crown Princess Beatrix, is vociferous in her attitude. She is an International Trustee of the World Wildlife organization (so are the husbands of the two aforementioned queens, Prince Philip of England and Prince Bernhard of the Netherlands), and at a recent congress presented a resolution she herself had drafted! In it she appealed specifically and directly to all women, saying, "women are considered to have special responsibility for preserving the natural heritage of mankind." She asked them to refrain from wearing or buying any object or garment made of any part of an endangered animal, citing crocodile, otter, leopard, snow leopard, tiger, ocelot, jaguar, cheetah, python, and vicuna as ten species in acute danger of complete extinction merely because of the dictates of fashion.

2. Your Household Wash

Probably no one item brought the household ecological problem so sharply into focus as did washing detergents. What's more, detergents have done it *twice*—and both times the public outcry caused constructive steps to be taken.

The first trouble was the foam. Suds were found to be billowing up in places nobody wanted them to billow—on a glass of tap water, at the edge of a stream, around the land entrance of a marsh, or across a tranquil pond. In some places foam built up several feet high: then wind scattered the banks of foam, blowing it in tightly bubbled lumps, to disfigure and kill off the plants and greenery in the surrounding landscape.

It was not only out in the open that the foam was a problem. Housewives found suds bubbling up through their sink drains, or rising over the toilet bowls of their high-rise apartments.

Detergent manufacturers soon began removing the suds-producing agents from their products—after admitting that these agents had been put in only because the average housewife equated suds with cleansing power! That such an association had no validity was beside the point in the detergent sellers' minds—suds helped the product to sell, so suds were added. When the truth became evident, they were promptly taken out and the scourge of the sudsing rivers abated within a short time. All was again quiet on the detergent front—until the phosphates scandal came to light.

Here again, the problem was an additive that was vaunted as a cleansing superagent. Unfortunately, it also proved to be a super-feeder of algae: an overproduction of algae in the waterways causes overconsumption of oxygen, leaving an insufficient supply for fish and other marine life. The result? Thriving algae, dead fish, decimated marine life. This was serious pollution—and again the culprit was the detergent industry.

As this is being written, the detergent companies are working overtime to find viable solutions to the problem. One would like to think they are genuinely concerned with the environment—but one knows perfectly well that their real concern is directed toward sales and profit.

These experiences indicate, however, that the housewife of the seventies is not the easily sold creature she was believed to be during the fifties. Should any company try to promote a phony solution, the ruse will not work for long. The many watchdog agencies and societies (listed later in this book) are far more in tune with the needs and moods of the people, in particular those of the housewife.

Yet even today, reading some of the detergent ads, I get the impression that the feverish force with which the washing compounds are said to attack the clothes would surely wear out normal clothes worn by normal families. Even the brand names given to many of these products signal battering-ram force. Is this really necessary?

Enzymes, a relatively recent "miracle" additive, have been proved to be powerful skin and mucous-membrane irritants. When found in their proper place in the biological world, enzymes are plant or animal proteins acting as catalysts and directing the action of water on other proteins. When found in detergents, commercial enzymes again direct the action of water and enable it to "lift off" dirt with greater speed.

The trouble is that this self-same power can go to work on the hands that are washing the clothes, causing inflamed spots or

rashes that resemble forms of eczema. A more serious inflammation can be suffered from breathing in enzyme-loaded dust; here
the irritant can be introduced not only into the nasal passages but
into the lungs, too.

On the other side of the fence, some of the new banners and
slogans of the so-called "clean" detergents are misleading, too. For
example, the authoritative ring of "biodegradability" sounds
impressive and, presumably, can sway the undecided buyer. The
truth of the matter is, however, that nearly *all* detergents have
been biodegradable since the mid-1960's. What's "new" about it is
that the term influences shoppers.

The phosphate ratings (at this time of writing) aren't too
reliable, either, for there are several different kinds of phosphates
and to date only some of them are counted in the ratings. Thus, a
detergent rated "low" in phosphates may be low in only *one or
two kinds* of phosphates, but loaded to the gills with other kinds.

The detergent and cleansing agent picture will change, hopefully, from month to month for some time to come. A number of
factors and ingredients are still questionable, in terms of both
value and potential pollution danger. Further, commercial compe-
tition is going to make today's loser into tomorrow's winner, and
vice versa. Therefore it is not feasible to list here a selection of
today's best and safest washing detergents. I can, however, list
some harmless washing practices and some ingredients that may be
substituted for the dubious detergents. All these methods place
heavy emphasis on the world's truly "magical" cleanser—soap.

Yes, good old-fashioned soap is about as old as civilization. It is
dependable and durable, but made of natural ingredients that
bacteria can handle—it's always a threat to dirt and germs, but
never to mankind or the environment. It breaks down beautifully
in city sewage systems and it does not poison anyone or anything
as it decomposes.

What's more, it cleans very well, too—even in hard water, if the
right methods are used and minimal care is taken.

Anyone inclined to dismiss soap as outmoded would do well to
reconsider the merits of a product still used by surgeons. As they
begin their preoperative cleansing routine, they scrub their hands

with soap, not the latest fancy foamer. Also, far more skin irritations, allergies, and nasal passage inflammations are caused by detergents than by soap. And when I say soap, I'm talking about the straight stuff—not the powders or bars that are "beefed up" or "boosted" by formula numbers or additives that are of dubious value and often poisonous. (I know no one should eat a bar of soap, but try telling that to an adventurous two-year-old or a rambunctious puppy. If they chomp into a plain bar of soap, they bubble and perhaps vomit it back up and emerge from the experience wiser and unharmed. If they tackle a boosted soap bar, they can become desperately ill.)

Now as to methods: I'm sure we all know how to wash clothes with soap, be it in cake, powdered, or flake form. In recent times, however, washing with soap has been so associated with hand-laundering that many people have forgotten (while perhaps younger people don't even know) that soap can be used for heavy duty wash as well.

WASHING MACHINES

For anyone switching from detergents to soap, home economics experts have suggested they run their wash through a prewashing cycle, so as to rid the clothes of detergents left from previous launderings. This is the suggested routine:

1. Put clothes in washer, add water and ½ cup washing soda. Run through a regular wash cycle and repeat until there are no more suds.

2. Having gotten rid of all residual detergent traces, the actual wash can now start (of course, if laundry items are new, or were never previously laundered, you can skip step 1). The sequence to remember is: first clothes, then water, then soda, and lastly soap. You put the laundry in the washer, let in the water, add anywhere from ¼ to ⅓ cup of washing soda, and get it well dissolved. Then comes the soap, about 1½ cups—and there you have it.

Should the water in your area be very hard, you may want to add ½ cup soda to the first rinse cycle. If you have soft water, on the other hand, you may not need to bother with soda at all except for removing leftover detergent.

Another method is as follows:

Add washing soda (approximately ⅓ cup) to the water as the washing machine is filling. Put in clothes after soda has dissolved, and then add 1½ cups soap powder or flakes.

This method may require a ¼ cup of washing soda to be added to the first rinse if the water is hard.

Another rinse trick to remember is the addition of vinegar. This is especially good on things like dark cottons or dark socks, which can develop peculiar white streaks from insufficient rinsing or adverse water conditions. When using a machine, add a generous dash of vinegar—½ to a full cup. When hand-laundering, less will do, of course.

HAND-LAUNDERING

Turning to hand-laundering as opposed to the large family machine wash, using up small pieces of leftover soap is worth considering here. Soap-holding gadgets with a long handle accommodate the slivers and fragments of almost-finished soap cakes. These are placed under the running water as the basin or sink fills and perhaps allowed to sit and soak for a few minutes. Then a vigorous swizzling (that's what the long handle is for) works enough dissolved soap into the water—and there's the perfect solution for all the hand-washables. (It's also the perfect solution for all the little bits of soap that you can't use normally any more but are too thrifty to throw away.)

Another way to use soap cake remnants is the soap-jelly method. Collect the soap pieces in a wide-necked jar, and when it is slightly more than half full, pour boiling water (or extremely hot water, if you're using a glass jar) and fill the receptacle up to the brim. Let this mixture sit and blend (you can give it a stir or two to help the process along). The resulting jelly is another perfect cleanser for delicate hand laundry. If you pick an attractive earthenware pot in which to make the mixture, it can sit decoratively on a bathroom shelf, close at hand whenever stockings need rinsing out or a light garment requires quick laundering.

Small pieces of leftover soap can also be put into a plastic bag with holes punched in it, and given to a child to bubble up his or her bath. This uses up soap, recycles a plastic bag, and washes the younger generation, all in one fell swoop.

From washing to ironing, momentarily—did you know that excellently pure water for your steam iron can be obtained simply by melting down the ice that forms in your freezer? This distilled water is also good in car batteries, incidentally.

Since this book is intended to be realistic, I readily acknowledge that there are cases where detergents will continue to be used—in the hand-laundering of woolen knits, for example. As a matter of fact, detergents first came into steady use in the wool industry, where they were used to get the fat content out of the wool itself.

Also, there are housewives who, by preference or perhaps personal conviction, will continue to use detergents in their washing machines—but not indiscriminately, we hope. Using too much detergent in a load of wash is as bad for the clothes (and eventually the budget) as it is for the environment, for it causes unnecessary stress to the fibers, making them break down and grow old before their time. Ruining clothes in this manner makes no sense at all, economic or ecological.

Besides controlling the amount of detergent you use per wash-load, you should keep informed on the progress made by the detergent makers themselves. Citizen group reports, rather than boastful ads, tend to carry the truth, and local newspapers or civic club publications should be encouraged to carry all such informative items. Consumer protection agencies, too, are supposed to keep tabs on progress and put out news items. Don't ignore these bits of news as "boring" or "irrelevant": remember, we're all on this planet together, and everyone's household wash is part of the earth's water cycle.

3. Household Cleaners

One of the best ways of cutting down on packages, nonbiodegradables, and just plain trash—as well as cooling off the manufacturers a bit—is to substitute natural, multiple-purpose cleaning agents for those that come in spray cans and bottles. For instance:

If you buy a small antique washstand with a marble top, or have a pair of block marble bookends, lemon, water, and borax will polish up the marble. Don't invest in a full container of commercial marble cleanser; after all, the item won't need cleaning and polishing every day of the week; it is only too easy to clutter your shelves with long-unused specialist cleansers if you don't know the long-standing cleaning agents, those basic standbys that are always good to know.

Whether you use them in a pinch (when you've run out of the commercial product) or prefer them on a permanent basis is a question of personal choice. The ingredients used are natural, their cleansing powers equally so—many of them are less wearing on the object being cleaned than a commercial product would be, and therefore they help keep your things in good condition longer. (This is the case when using salt rather than corrosive chemicals to clean drains, for example.)

To get down to specifics, let us start in the kitchen.

KITCHEN CLEANSERS

Salt is one of nature's strongest and best all-purpose cleansers and purifiers. It has antiseptic and disinfectant properties, along with the abrasive cleansing ones. It can be used as a cleaning agent on its own, or in combination with other common kitchen ingredients. Two other common cleaning agents are water and vinegar.

A solution of salt and water will effectively rinse out bottles, pans, or any other receptacles you wish to rid of all traces of soap or detergent. You can scour with salt, too. And you can clean, clear, and disinfect drains with it.

If you use a dishwasher, you'll find you can use far less dishwashing detergent than the directions call for. The hotter the water, the better, of course—and should you make a mistake and add too much detergent, getting an overabundance of suds, scatter salt on them and they'll break up and disappear.

(As for hand-washed dishes, whether you use soap or detergent [keeping the latter to a minimum here, too] : *wear gloves.* They are worth every penny they cost and it's not just a question of "beautiful hands." There's also the question of overdrying the skin, not to mention the crop of rashes and other skin problems that have been caused by too much exposure to detergent.)

Keep salt in mind: it is a household staple, as are other items mentioned in the following recipes, and therefore always at hand when the need arises.

DRAINS

A handful or two of salt followed by boiling water does an excellent job of cleaning or clearing the average sink or basin drain.

For clogged drains, change to bicarbonate of soda. Pour in a handful of it, followed by ½ cup of vinegar. Then replace the plug and close the drain. Let it sit for a while; then let water run through it. Finally, if you like, give it one last salt-and-hot-water treatment.

SINKS

You can scour a sink with salt. This is well worth remembering if you are going to use the sink for washing vegetables or preparing foods in any manner. A sink scoured with salt is clean and disinfected—and without your having used any poisonous substance. Salt is not toxic, as are most bleaches, scouring powders, and so forth.

PANS

Suppose you've let something cook down too far and too long, and now there's a blackened and rock-hard mess inside. First remove as much as you can of the burned particles of food and then fill the pan with *cold* water. Add salt, and be generous in doing so—½ cup, say, for a small pan. You can also add a piece of onion, if you have one.

Let the pan sit with the cold water, salt, and optional onion for at least twelve hours (overnight is a good idea.) Then bring it to a boil very slowly, over a low flame. Let it boil for five minutes. Then set the pan aside and let the water cool. When it is completely cold, drain it off and clean and scour the pan in the usual manner.

A pan that is merely stained will benefit from a mixture of water and apple peelings and cores brought to a good, strong boil for as long as it takes to remove the marks.

Aluminum pots, by the way, brighten up inside when any citrus is cooked in them—but I view these pans with a rather jaundiced eye. Followers of natural health foods and medicines reject aluminum cookware, and their attitude is credible in view of the many recipes that must be cooked in neutral receptacles, such as enamel-covered pots and pans.

COPPER PANS

There are both copper pans and copper-*bottomed* pans, and either variety can be cleaned by the following methods.

For a quick once-over, a lemon half dipped in salt and lustily scrubbed over the copper surface will do the trick. Polish dry with a soft cloth.

To make a copper cleansing paste, mix:

½ cup white vinegar
¼ cup table salt
¼ cup scouring powder

If the copper is very dirty or badly tarnished, you can use a steel wool pad when you work the mixture over the copper surface. If not, a damp cloth will do. Rinse off with very hot water.

A paste made of equal parts of hot vinegar, flour, and salt also cleans copper rather well.

KITCHEN STAINS

Various food stains, such as egg on cutlery or vegetable juice on counter tops, can be removed by dipping a damp cloth into table salt or baking soda and then rubbing it firmly over the stain. Ashes, too, can be used in a similar spot-cleaning manner, so if you've just rounded up all the ashtrays in the house, keep a sharp lookout for spots that need removing.

PLASTIC WARE

Scouring plastic cups and plates with steel wool or abrasive powders risks damaging the surface and causing permanent discoloration. Instead, use baking soda, dampened to a paste with water. Apply it with a sponge or brush: if the stains are bad ones, you can let it sit and work a while before rinsing off.

SILVERWARE

Intricately patterned or antique silverware should always be cleaned in the conventional way, with commercial polish, soft cloth, and lots of patience (and gloves are a necessity on this job). Simple flatware, however, with no deep recesses or ornate curlicues, can be quickly cleaned by the following methods.

1. Crush a sheet of aluminum foil and place it at the bottom of a glass baking dish. Arrange cutlery pieces on it so that they do not touch each other. Fill the baking dish with boiling water and sprinkle two tablespoons of baking soda for every quart of water used.

Five minutes should be more than ample for removing all the tarnish without removing too much of the silver.

It is true, of course, that you are removing an infinitesimal layer of the silver whenever you use methods like this. However, the conventional method of polishing silver rubs off that same infinitesimal layer.

Salt, water, and foil is said to have much the same effect as the above-described combination. For more thorough cleaning, though, the following method is more effective.

2. Here you *do* need an aluminum pan! You also need:

1 quart water
1 tablespoon bicarbonate of soda
1 tablespoon salt

Bring this mixture to a boil in the pan. Drop your flatware into it as it boils, doing only a few pieces at a time. Let them boil for three minutes, then take them out and let them drain on a soft cloth, drying them to a shine with a second cloth.

Don't overcrowd the pot: it can confuse the issue as to which pieces have already done their three minutes and which still have time to go; also, it can lower the temperature of the liquid, thus also lowering its efficiency.

FURNITURE CLEANSERS AND POLISHES

Moving into the rest of the house, let's tackle that piece of marble first.

MARBLE

Cut a fresh lemon in half. Hold it within a cloth, dipping with cut edge down into warm water and then borax. Rub the marble surface with this lemon-pad; then polish it with a soft dry cloth.

BRASS

Although brass can also be cleaned with the mixtures given for copper, it has a formula of its own.

Mix equal parts of salt and flour. Add enough vinegar to this mixture to make a stiff paste. Apply it to the brass, covering the surface well, and allow the paste to dry. Then rinse it off quickly and wipe the surface dry with a soft cloth.

If the brass objects you want to clean are rings—from café curtains, for example—then the paste method is unnecessary. Drop the rings into a solution of vinegar and water instead. After they have soaked, a light scrub and a brisk rub to dry should finish the job nicely.

CHROME AND STAINLESS STEEL

The chrome and stainless steel polish is actually so simple as to sound unbelievable. It is merely a cloth that has been dipped in flour—ordinary, everyday white flour. (Actually, it's probably better at cleaning metal than it is at nourishing human beings, since we are dealing with the bleached and refined stuff!)

All you do is dip a dry cloth into some flour and then use it for shining up faucets, tricycle handlebars, cabinet edges, or whatever else is made of stainless steel or chrome that is no longer at its shining best.

PLASTIC TILES

Plastic tiles are best cleaned with a solution of vinegar and water. It's the vinegar that prevents the "spotting" effect as the tile dries.

GLASS

Hard water area residents are usually familiar with the problem of spotting on glass, and crystal, too. They will find that adding vinegar to the wash or rinse water (be the glass a window pane or a flower vase) will eliminate or at least tone down the problem.

Another window-cleaning weapon is newspaper. A wad of it dipped in a vinegar-and-water solution is a good standby. (Newspaper will also do the trick if you run out of cleaning cloths when tackling copper or brass.)

Crystal, whether in the form of wine glasses, paperweights, or chandeliers, is always best cleaned in a solution of one part vinegar to three parts water. If the crystal is very dirty, you can use several different baths, dipping the object into bath number one to get the worst of the dirt off, and then swishing it in and out of baths two, three, and even four.

Use *only* vinegar and water; do *not* use a final rinse of water only. If the crystal is very dirty and/or intricately cut, a soft brush may be used during the first and second baths. Two baths is a normal routine, three for very dirty objects. Four leans toward the persnickety, although it could be possible if you had a great many crystal objects—say, the myriad pieces from a big chandelier—and they were really grimy. Still, you'd do better to clean half the piece in three baths and then do the second half with three fresh baths.

After removing the crystal from the final bath, do *not* wipe or attempt to dry. Either hang it up (if it is a chandelier portion) or place it on a clean cloth and let it air-dry.

CANE, RATTAN

Furniture and matting made of these tropical materials can be cleaned and refreshed by very simple methods. If a cane chair is looking the worse for wear after a summer's usage, shine it generously with a vinegar-and-water solution (equal parts of each liquid). Brush while it's still wet and shine it with the remaining liquid, then place it in a windy or at least drafty spot.

When merely cleaning, use a water-and-salt solution—1 table-spoon salt per quart of water used. Heat the liquid till lukewarm (or merely add the salt to lukewarm water) and brush it on to cane or rattan furniture. Dry out of doors, if possible, on a warm day.

POLISHED WOOD

An easy formula for daily (or weekly) "top polishing" of all polished wood surfaces is again a vinegar-and-water mix. The proportions are ½ cup vinegar to 1 gallon water, but I don't think this is crucial. Unless you have a mansion full of polished surfaces to shine, you can just as well use a dash or two of vinegar in a cup of water.

Dip a cloth into this mixture and then wring it out until it's just slightly damp. Run it over all the polished surfaces and follow with a swift swipe with a soft cloth. And that's that.

For more serious (and less frequent) polishing, there is:

ALL-PURPOSE FURNITURE POLISH
½ cup vinegar
½ cup methylated spirits (rubbing alcohol)
1 cup linseed oil

You'll have to shake these ingredients together every time you use them, so just pour them into a bottle, give it a good initial shake, and store.

This polish is excellent for all polished wood surfaces and many painted ones, too. For the latter, apply *very* thinly and always try it out in a small corner first to make sure it won't strip the paint! (To take the finger marks off painted surfaces, incidentally, try rubbing a slice of potato over them—it often works like a charm and avoids a messy soap-and-water operation.)

If hot cups or alcoholic drinks have left rings on polished wood surfaces, reach for the nearest ash-filled ashtray and dip a moistened cloth into it. Then rub the ring vigorously with this; it usually dispels the ring immediately and you can polish the surface later.

Nor should one forget, when thinking of blemishes, the use of nut meats to obliterate scratches on stained or polished wood. Pecans and walnuts both work. The thing is to match your nut meat to the wood and then rub the meat over the whitened scratch. This will darken the scratch mark until it "disappears."

LEATHER FURNITURE

This is another tried and true recipe that, when lightly applied and well rubbed in, will both refresh the appearance of the leather and help keep it smooth and supple.

A point to remember when following recipes that use linseed oil and similar items that need to be heated, is to take the necessary precautions. Most oils—certainly linseed, for one—are *very* flammable. They should be heated carefully: put the oil in a pan *inside another pan* which has water in it.

LEATHER POLISH AND RENEWER

1 cup linseed oil
1 cup vinegar

Bring the linseed oil to boiling point (using two pans, as described above). Remove from the fire and cool. Then add the vinegar. Mix and keep in a bottle. Always shake the mixture before using.

Apply this mixture sparingly to any leather that has gotten shabby or stained. Put it on with a soft cloth and polish with a second soft cloth.

Sometimes a light touch of vaseline or mineral oil, applied and buffed with woolen cloths (the cut-up rags of an old sweater are perfect for this) will really do the trick on leather.

PATENT LEATHER

Patent leather responds to the vaseline treatment as well, but it also shines up nicely with a light application of milk! Dab on the milk with a small piece of cotton or cloth, and buff well with a dry, soft cloth.

To round off this section, here is a recipe for an all-purpose wax that is long-lasting and sound.

ALL-PURPOSE WAX
Beeswax
Turpentine

The proportions depend on the consistency of wax that you prefer, but a good general guide is two parts turpentine to one part wax.

First chop up a lump of beeswax, then put the pieces in any kind of container and place it in a pan of hot water on the stove. Heat it until the wax is melted, then remove it from the stove. When the wax is cooler, but still liquid, add the turpentine. *Cold* turpentine, that is. *Never* mess around with turpentine near heat or an open flame, because you'll risk blowing everything to smithereens.

Mix well and allow it to cool. You will then have genuine, workable, all-purpose wax.

TIN

Tin objects can be cleaned by rubbing with a cloth soaked in gasoline. Leave the object to dry, then rub with a cloth soaked in hot beer, giving a good buff and polish.

JEWELRY CLEANING

Intricate, gem-studded pieces of jewelry do require the care of a professional jeweler, but there are a number of simple home routines that will keep most personal jewelry in good and sparkling order in between times. This goes for costume jewelry pieces especially, so that the procedures and ingredients are well worth knowing.

NECKLACES

Necklaces—no matter what they are made of—should *never* be dipped into water or any other liquid. It weakens and rots the holding thread and increases its chances of breaking.

Therefore, necklaces have to be freshened up by the dry-cleaning method. Using a soft brush, work dry baking soda in and around all the pieces of the necklace. The brushwork plus the soda will take off any dulling film that has accumulated. Finish by rubbing the necklace with a soft cloth or a chamois.

AMETHYSTS, CRYSTAL, EMERALDS, RUBIES, SAPPHIRES, TOPAZES, AND TURQUOISES

All these stones, when set in rings or pins, may be washed in warm, soapy water and gently rubbed or brushed until clean. In the case of exceptional dirt, a few drops of ammonia can be added to the water.

Rinse in clear water and place on clean, lint-free cloth to dry.

COPPER JEWELRY

Copper bangles are popular not only for their attractive appearance, but for their reputed power to alleviate pains of rheumatism and arthritis. To keep any piece of copper jewelry bright and shining, wash it in soap and water. Then plunge it into a solution of two parts vinegar to one part salt. Take it out and dry with a soft cloth.

COSTUME JEWELRY

Go easy on costume jewelry. The safest method is the dry-cleaning one—back to your soft brush and baking soda. Many pieces of costume jewelry can be washed, of course, but I'd suggest warm water for both wash and rinse, mild suds and above all, *speed.* You don't want to soften the cement that holds the stones in place.

Tarnish can sometimes be removed by dabbing the piece with a wad of cotton soaked in alcohol and then wiping with a soft cloth.

DIAMONDS

Diamonds are tough and can be subjected to *very* hot water—even boiling—without suffering at all. The best method is to give them a good rub-and-scrub in hot soapy water with a drop of ammonia added. Rinse in very hot, clear water, then dip them into alcohol and place on lint-free surface to dry.

You can use a toothbrush with toothpaste or powder to clean your diamonds, too. Simply brush the diamond with the toothbrush and paste or powder and then rinse it under hot water.

If you have a ring or a pin that is composed of diamonds plus some other kind of stone, use the cleaning method suited to the more delicate of the gems, remembering that whatever the combination, the diamond is bound to be the toughest.

GOLD AND SILVER

Gold can be washed with warm, soapy water and it can also be given a shine with toothpaste! This method works on silver jewelry, too. A final polish with a piece of chamois leather is a good idea.

Mind you, this refers to gold and silver, not gold plate or silver plate, since plating can wear off rather quickly if not given the gentlest of treatment.

JADE, JET AND MOTHER-OF-PEARL

Warm, soapy water, quick washing, clear-water rinsing, and thorough drying are the answers. Speed is of the essence and *no soaking,* which is why those delicate fruit knives and forks with the mother-of-pearl handles should never, never be put into a dishwasher.

OPALS

No water, *ever.* Opals are delicate and porous and need protection. This can easily be given them by rubbing any pure, *lightweight* oil into them (glycerine is excellent) and then polishing them with a lint-free soft cloth or chamois.

PEARLS

Have them cleaned and restrung professionally and often. However, I have known of owners who kept their pearl necklaces in a box of rice between visits to the jewelers! It is aid to be good for them—as is wearing them often, for the oils of the skin are beneficial to pearls. The same goes for pearl rings and pins.

PLATINUM

This is another tough metal, so very hot water and soap will do it no harm.

And whatever you're cleaning, by whatever method—remember to wear your gloves.

4.   Recycling Your Discards

The most obvious thing to make out of discards is money. This can be done in many different ways and at varying levels of profitability. The profit made can be money saved, or money earned, or both.

The sums involved can also vary. (I think the $38 *million* recently earned by the inventor of a rice-hull converting process is encouraging.) Not all of us are inventors, of course, but the savable and earnable sums are still there, certainly within our more modest grasp.

However much big business may drag its feet about recycling at first, eventually recycling will *have* to become part of almost all industry. It is no longer a question of choice; the earth's resources are finite, and we are going to have to learn to reuse them.

At a day-long program in New York City which brought 500 government people and private citizens together to discuss the prospects and problems of recycling, Senator Gaylord Nelson of Wisconsin had some provocative facts and figures to cite.

"Petroleum-to-fuel industry is expected to last only another 70 or 80 years," the Senator stated. "Many other vital materials—tin, tungsten, helium—are already running short and will be nearly exhausted by the end of this century."

These figures mean the end will occur within the lifetimes of many readers, and there are other materials—copper, lead, nickel, zinc, gold, silver, manganese, aluminum, and platinum among them—whose existence in the raw are not expected to last much longer, either.

Therefore, the sooner more people realize that there's gold in them thar garbage hills, the sooner the full recycling process will get going. Whether we like the philosophical implications or not, our civilization turns on money: when something becomes a probable money-maker, people become interested in its possibilities.

Unfortunately, under many facets of the present industrial and commercial setup, there is no forceful rationale for recycling. It is quite literally cheaper, at present, to make throwaway containers. In fact, this point was made in a series of advertisements ostensibly announcing the opening of recycling centers.

The ads said that since businesses were already set up to make discardable containers, it would cost "money and jobs" to change the system. Possibly true enough—but just how does an attitude like that stack up against the facts of finite raw material? And I personally don't believe the "jobs" part of the statement; that has all the earmarks of a psychological stab suggested by a motivation-minded image-maker.

What it all means is that, *right now*, it would cost the company and its shareholders money (the latter in the form of lower dividends) to reform the company's *modus operandi* into a recycling operation. But what I want to know is: *What about the long run?* What's going to happen when the metals run out? Wouldn't it be better to spend time and effort now and avoid the panic and eventual desolation later?

Admittedly, there are companies that have set up recycling centers, and there are sure to be more and more of them in the immediate future. As raw materials become scarcer, recycling will pay. Many corporations are no doubt sincerely motivated; others are not.

A rule of thumb when judging the sincerity of a company's recycling actions is: *How easy do they make it for the public to use?* After all, when a company markets a new product, they just about stand on their corporate heads trying to attract customers' attention. All this effort is expended because they sincerely want to sell a product. And that's the way industry will have to approach the marketing of recycling centers, too.

As yet, such efforts have been somewhat below the mark. As one ecologically minded young man put it: "You practically have to gift wrap your discards before they'll even look at them," and he certainly has a point. It is up to the consumer, saith commerce, to clean, sort, pack up, and cart over the cans, bottles, and what-have-you to the recycling center; under these circumstances, only those passionately involved in the ecological movement are going to continue for more than the few weeks of first enthusiasm. Therefore, unless they make it easier and speedier and far more efficient, I'm afraid the recycling efforts of container-making companies will have to be regarded with underlying suspicion.

Apart from the centers set up by commercial companies, there have also been community and charity-run drives. Most of these are well-meaning, perhaps limited in scope, but nonetheless of good example, but they are often uninformed and undisciplined. It is unfortunate that do-goodism can be confusing; club members picking up cans along a highway are to be commended for their zeal, but the country's future will not be solved by such isolated instances. Those same members should persist in the effort, in every way—politically and economically.

If you think about it for a moment, you will realize that the much-respected antique business is, in its way, recycling used goods. A less revered business, but probably one of equal vintage, is the "thrift shop"—an institution that could do with considerable general expansion.

For many years, women wealthy enough to have extensive new wardrobes each season have been selling off their discards. Surely this form of trade could be widened. All it needs is social acceptance—and that's easier to come by when reason and necessity join hands.

What better way to recycle items such as children's clothes, for example, than by selling them? Children grow so fast that a "good winter coat" will usually serve only one winter. When I was very young I attended a school where the headmistress, on her own initiative, had organized a "clothes-swapping" center. As children grew out of clothes that were still in good condition, their items went into the school store to serve another child's needs. Perhaps it would speed interest in such matters if someone were to coin new, more exciting names for thrift shops.

Or perhaps, it would be better to rename them what they were originally called: secondhand stores or shops. The honesty of statement might well appeal to the newly forming ecological conscience. Social acceptance of the secondhand store will also be helped by other changing values. Constant acquisition of new material goods was, for a time, regarded in some circles as a mark of superiority. Fortunately, this type of consumer madness is today recognized for what it is—a sign of personal insecurity.

Apart from clothes, furniture, and objects of art—what else could be sold in secondhand shops? The answer is just about anything: what may be useless—an encumbrance in fact—to one person may be just the thing another was looking for. Therefore, what we need are exchange centers, where the one can dump his discard and the other find his treasure.

Take the matter of office supplies. Businesses do, from time to time, move their quarters. This involves an enormous amount of clearing up and cleaning out: old envelopes, forms no longer used, half-empty boxes of stationery, paper clips, carbon sheets are all thrown out. The company no longer needs them or wants them; and yet they are not really garbage at all. All that is needed is a market for these still perfectly usable supplies, and it quite definitely does exist.

An inking-out stamp or a few strokes of a felt-tipped pen can obliterate a company name or logo from stationery; if such merchandise were cheaply available, there are needy college students, struggling writers, and others who would use it. As to printed forms, paper can be recycled. There have been businesses in this field for years. General office supplies (pencils, staples, etc.) should certainly be resold as they often are now, if only to avoid adding to the ever-growing problem of garbage disposal.

What it takes to get the scheme going is the profit incentive. Just as new life styles are becoming a recognizable portion of society today, so new shopping styles and centers are emerging as necessary, viable—and profitable.

On the household level, there are of course many unwanted objects that might be sold off secondhand, but other avenues too are open to your discards. Neighborhood "white elephant" sales (or even individual garage sales) can raise money for all sorts of objects. This latter form can bring about tax benefits to the donor, and details on such matters need to be checked at the local level. A few phone calls are all it takes to benefit you, the eventual receiver of the goods, and the balance of living things.

For every old bed, or chair, or dress, or pair of shoes that does *not* land on the garbage heap, there is that much less that has to be burned and disposed of, that much less space taken up by the remaining fragments.

There is much recycling that can be done within a household, too. All sorts of things that come into our homes can have multiple uses—so why not take advantage of them, thus saving ourselves money as we help save and safeguard the environment?

The following suggestions and examples are merely a small random selection from among thousands. You will find that once you start thinking in terms of recycling, even objects as yet labeled "disposable" take on added life cycles. Never mind such terms as "permanent" or "disposable": using an object until it is really "worn out" will take us far along the balanced way.

For example, until recently plastic can covers were used for the duration of the can's kitchen life. Once the foodstuff in question was used up—say, coffee or cottage cheese—container and top were thrown out. However, some realized that the plastic top is a useful mess-saving coaster for putting underneath cooking oil bottles (to eliminate a greasy ring on the kitchen shelf), under a potted plant, or, for that matter, under glasses or cups— particularly those used by small children. Plastic tops can also continue their useful careers as covers—over pet-food cans, a cup holding egg whites, or leftovers of any nature. They can also protect the early days of seedlings pushing their way up in an unbreakable pot formed from that same plastic can; thus covered, the pot becomes a miniature greenhouse.

Furniture legs that dig into rugs can also be made less damaging by slipping a can cover under them; slipped between records, the plastic discs can hold LP's upright and categorized in a bookcase.

The same goes for all those free plastic bags one keeps getting—on bread, dry cleaning, potato chips, and what-have-you. If the original contents were sticky (jelly beans) or smelly (of dry-cleaning fluid), rinse the plastic bag thoroughly, dry, and then reuse it inside out. Otherwise, merely remove the original contents—you may get only one reuse out of a bag, but in any case the garbage rate is slowed and your pennies saved. *Buying* plastic bags does seem like financial foolishness when so many are given away free.

With all those plastic bags you can wrap sandwiches, store or freeze food, wrap clothing up for seasonal storage, keep stockings tidy and snag-free in a drawer, carry a goldfish (in water) to a new home, stash laundry, or keep clothes to be ironed or mended. You can also cover books (good for school books and sticky fingers), and line shelf or drawer and not feel wasteful when you throw the lining out and put in a fresh one.

The idea of an "Ecology Closet" has great appeal. In it you would store all such reusable items as paper, string, boxes, cartons, plastic containers, ribbons, yarn, fabric—to provide materials for recycling as the need arises. A whole closet is not necessarily needed; a basement shelf or a section of a cupboard will suffice, or even a nice deep drawer.

Creative processes can be brought into play here, too, for to manage all one's gift wrapping from the contents of the "ecology shelf" can stir the imagination and hone personal ability. Scissors, paste, and ideas can produce marvelous results. I once saw an extremely showy selection of Christmas packages, all done up in newsprint and bright red ribbon. I also remember a backyard picnic where the "tablecloth" was a selection of a preschooler's art—the child herself chose the drawings and paintings, which had been done on variously sized pieces of paper, and, with a little adult help, taped them together.

Recycling objects for children's use is doubly rewarding. Ordinary brown paper bags become comic, individual faces with a few basic strokes of crayon or pen, or three-dimensional ima- ginings when paste or added paper come into use. Contrasting paper (or other material) can make a collage out of a parcel—or a pirate's face, complete with eyepatch and moustache. Humor, fantasy, color, and enjoyment all become part of the pleasure of gift giving and gift wrapping; there is more, I think, to an ecology closet than the recyclable objects that first meet the eye.

Jars and bottles and other glass objects are commonly on view as unsightly litter. (Again, bacteria find glass inedible, and it can be broken down only by slow chemical action.) The bottle manufacturers have realized that such "leftovers" are bad for their image, and so the recycling of bottles has recently received some small amount of publicity. Yet here again, the whole program needs an encouraging push from the profit incentive. Returned glass is melted down and then made into new bottles. This has been going on for years, a small and relatively unknown area of business activity. I suspect that a better price paid for used bottles might help, or a tax on "new" new bottles, or a tax-exemption or aid of some kind on new bottles made from old—or, most likely, all three.

Meanwhile, empty jars and bottles can be put to good use in the home, too. Sizable ones with good screw-caps make excellent cannisters. Ordinary jars can be made to match; paint will decorate the cap, and the glass too, if desired.

As a matter of fact, painted bottles were all the rage during the Victorian era, most of them for toilet articles, lavender water, or smelling salts. What is to prevent an assortment of mayonnaise jars from becoming equally decorative?

If you cannot paint pretty patterns or flower pictures, you could get the effect you want by making up a stencil, or copying from a design you have seen in a book or magazine. Simple bands of color look attractive. Or dip the jars—or just their tops—into paint and then let them stand to dry—you might get some unusual effects that way.

In all Victorian homes (and in a great many modern ones too) one of the bulwarks of the household machinery was the ragbag, a variously shaped and sized container wherein all clean fabric discards were stored—torn sheet remnants, the snippets left over from dressmaking, a tired apron, and similar items.

As many a car owner will testify, there is no better polishing rag than a soft, worn-out, clean hunk of T-shirt. Rags for applying waxes, or pastes, or cleansers, rags for washing windows, or for padding around a pipe, or making a comfortable lair in a carton for a new kitten or puppy, or sopping up an inkstain or making a temporary sling—all these and a thousand more can be fashioned from the ragbag collection.

That's from the *old* cloth ragbag, but from the new one—there is creativity and commerce, art and profit, all waiting for those who care enough to try. Quilts and the making of patchwork were both work and art in the lives of pioneer womenfolk. That art flourishes again today and industries grow colorfully from it. Quilts, skirts, kerchiefs, blouses—all sorts of garments can be made, enjoyed, given, and also profitably sold.

Rag dolls, dolls' clothes and doll house accessories are fashioned from pieces of fabric. A short while ago imaginative sleeping bags for children, designed and made by an enterprising housewife, turned into a full-fledged business.

On the household level it is unnecessary to turn *every* discard into a commercial venture, yet the uses of new rags are still legion. Some may be utilitarian (pot holders, pillow covers) and others may border on art: in "painting" with fabric and embroidery, only individual imagination sets the boundaries. Fabrics, yarns, and thread, combined with either weaving or sewing or even glue, can be made into pictures or pillows; in some cases, they also become exhibition pieces, as any crafts and embroidery enthusiast knows.

Leftover yarns should also have their niche in the ecology closet, for they not only combine with the ragbag contents but can be used creatively on their own, as well. A range of afghans—from simple squares to intricate patterns—takes care of scraps of yarn in a spectacular way. Yarn can also be used to tie small gifts, braid into trimming, or incorporate into the above-mentioned composite embroidery forms. There is also the braid doll, which can be quickly made up to amuse a small child.

Some of the most unlikely things do become art. For instance, you would not readily see art in a set of broken plates, would you? And yet, the unique and simple vision of a man in France created a fairy tale of a house. Day by day, he pieced together the shards he sought in the environs of his home in Chartres. The result is an incredible mosaic whose many scenes and themes cover the walls of his home. His widow, a very old lady now, still lives there, surrounded by the artistic creation that was her husband's labor of love and life.

Not many of us could carry such an activity so far, but I have seen homes in which pieces of broken china and pottery had been incorporated into a garden path. In another, colorful shards had been pressed into the rough-surfaced cement that surrounded a fireplace. And of course, those who don't have the time for such projects can always *donate* yarn, glass, and other such materials to nursery schools, children's hospitals, and such institutions as Goodwill Industries.

Part Two

PROTECTING YOURSELF INTERNALLY

5. Food for Health, Food for Thought

There is a difference between "health" foods and "healthful" foods—but that difference is often little more than one of image. The health food carries the connotation of faddist fancies and extremist regimes, skinny little old ladies nibbling alfalfa sandwiches. However, a sensible approach to healthful foods is not difficult to attain once you consider the facts.

There are four basic groups of foodstuffs, and we need adequate proportions daily from each group to maintain our health and energy. These four groups are:

1. *Meat and meat substitutes.* All the red meats, poultry, fish, eggs, beans, nuts, and refinements of these products such as peanut butter.

2. *Grains.* Foodstuffs made from wheat, oats, barley; or the grains themselves, such as rice.

3. *Dairy foods.* Milk and all the foodstuffs that can be made from it: cheese, cream, butter.

4. *Vegetables and fruit.*

When these foods are *normally* grown or raised, ripened, harvested, and prepared, there are no problems. It is in some of these very processes, however, that the trouble starts, for we have long been tampering with the growing, storage, and preparation of our food.

The reasons for such tampering were sensible at first: earlier generations discovered that meat could be kept for longer periods without rotting if it was smoked or dried or salted. Populations were thus able to keep from starving as they moved across meatless terrain, or survived a season of drought or a hard winter.

But today, although many of our more sophisticated methods of food preparation and preservation may be better, many are questionable, to say the least. The trend seems to be more and more toward the specialization of food that *keeps,* rather than food that nourishes.

I am referring to all the variously packaged alimentary items often termed "convenience" foods. Convenient they may well be—but just how nourishing are they? Never mind all those labels that say "enriched" and "vitamins added." If the product were properly raised, correctly harvested, and naturally prepared, there would be no need to add anything.

Few of us have the facilities or even the desire to grow our own food. However, there is still a selection of fresh foods on the market, and the more we make use of them, the better off we tend to be. I am quite aware that there are times when "convenience" foods are indeed convenient, and that's precisely when they should be used. But for regular day-to-day healthy nourishment, we are better served by the natural than by the contrived.

The old adage, "we should eat to live and not live to eat," is correct. Food is fuel, not compensation. It is what enables us to create energy and live our lives. To use food for any other purpose, to substitute it for some emotional lack, is to invite overweight or ill health.

This is not to say that one should not enjoy food. Quite the contrary. And fanaticism has no place at the healthy dinner table; those who eat meat should be tolerant of vegetarians, while those who swear by grain diets should allow their flesh-eating brethren the privilege of their choice. Eat with reason and enjoy what you fancy, allowing others to do the same.

Let us now turn to guidelines and specifics for each food group.

THE GRAINS

The hollowness of today's packaged food may well be most dramatically demonstrated in bread. A Nobel laureate has charged that commercial bread now has 60 percent fewer vitamins than it had twenty years ago. Another nutrition expert recently conducted an experiment in which he found that rats fed nothing but ordinary white bread died of malnutrition within three months!

This is hardly a picture of the "staff of life," is it? The three bread recipes that follow will produce truly nutritional mainstays. I have specified whole wheat flour throughout—it contains all the nutrients that have been pounded, bleached, and refined out of white flour—but you can mix and blend flours if you wish.

The three bread recipes work on three different principles. The first, which uses no leavening agent, rises because the yeasting action of the flour itself is triggered by the kneading and resting periods. There are many who claim this is the most healthful bread of all. The second recipe calls for yeast, which hastens the rising process. The third uses baking powder, which also rises but requires no kneading.

In the first two recipes the dough is placed into a *cold* oven and then the temperature is set. This is because of the yeasting process: the warming-up action of the oven gives the leavening a boost and insures that the loaf will cook through evenly. The third recipe calls for a preheated oven, which is necessary to capture the characteristic action of the baking powder.

Should you want thicker crusts to form on the outside of your loaves, brush them with oil or milk just before you pop them into the oven.

YEASTLESS BREAD
3 cups whole wheat flour
1 teaspoon salt
1 cup water

Put the flour and salt in a bowl and add the water, a bit at a time, working it into the flour with your fingers. You want to create a mixture that holds together and does not stick to the sides of the bowl.

Take the dough (now a cohesive lump) out of the bowl and place it on a flat working surface. Set your kitchen timer at 15 minutes, or note the time on a clock. For the next 15 minutes you are going to give that cohesive lump a real going-over.

Knead it firmly and constantly, flouring your hands (that is, dusting them with a light coating of flour) if the dough is too sticky. Add a dash of water if it is too dry. Above all, keep on kneading.

As you work the dough this way, it will become smoother and more unified. The kneading action is what provokes the flour's natural yeasting process into action.

When the 15 minutes' kneading period is over, put the dough into a bowl or a pan and cover it with a damp cloth. (A clean dishcloth, held under the faucet and then wrung out, is fine.) Put the covered dough aside and let it rise for about ten or twelve hours; it's a good idea to mix up a batch in the evening so it can do its major rising overnight.

At the end of this time take the dough out of the pan and give it another kneading. Seven to ten minutes will do it this time. Then shape your loaf and place it in an oiled pan. Check to see whether the cloth is still damp, refresh it with water and a wringing out if it needs it, and place it over the dough once more.

Set the covered dough aside and let it rise for two hours more. Then place it in a *cold* oven and set the temperature at 425°F.

This amount of dough will take just under an hour to bake. Test by plunging a straw or toothpick or some similar implement into the middle of the loaf. When it comes out clean, the bread is done.

This is a close-textured, chewy bread. Let it cool completely before slicing or eating it, so its full, rich flavor can come out.

The addition of honey or molasses not only sweetens bread but also keeps it fresher longer. This is a natural form of preservation that has no built-in health hazard. You can, if you wish, add a tablespoon of honey or molasses to the cup of water in the recipe above and either cut down slightly on the water or add some more flour. Breadmaking is not that critical when it comes to measurements, as you'll see after you've made a batch or two for yourself.

The next recipe is even more flexible, for here you can mix and add to either the wet mix or the dry mix.

YEAST BREAD
Wet Mix: 1 package yeast
        ½ cup lukewarm water

1 tablespoon honey and/or molasses
cold water

Dissolve the package of yeast in the lukewarm water, and when it is well blended add the honey, or molasses, or both. Then add enough cold water to make 1 cup of liquid.

Dry Mix: 1 teaspoon salt
3 cups whole wheat flour
OR
2 cups whole wheat flour and 1 cup of something else (say, ½ cup each of wheat germ and oats, or 1 cup rye flour, or any other grain or grain flour that takes your fancy)

Put the dry mix in a bowl and stir in the wet mix. (The best way to mix it is with your fingers.) Pat it into a ball of dough and put it aside to rise for one hour. It should increase its size by half.

Take the dough, flour your hands if necessary, and start kneading just as with with the first recipe. Give it a thorough 15-minute workout. Then set it aside to rise for one hour.

Place it in an oiled pan and into a *cold* oven. Set the oven temperature at 400°F. once the dough is inside. Bake for one hour, testing with a straw or toothpick after 45 minutes. Exact timing is impossible to give, as flours and ovens vary and so do the mixes.

If you use both honey and molasses in the wet mix, your bread will be quite sweet, but not cakelike.

You could also use part milk for the cup of liquid. If you enjoy baking bread, your imagination can really go to work on this recipe. Keep in mind that its basic proportions are:

1 cup liquid with 1 package yeast dissolved
3 cups flour with 1 teaspoon salt.

All the rest is up to you—and the vigor of your kneading!

On to the third recipe, and this time it's:

BAKING POWDER BREAD
1½ cups equal parts of milk and water mixed

3 cups whole wheat flour

3 teaspoons baking powder

First preheat the oven to 350°F.

Then mix and warm the milk and water. The proportion of milk to water may vary slightly, but the temperature must be warm.

Sift the flour and the baking powder into a bowl. Add the warm milk-and-water mixture and blend. Pour this stiff mixture directly into a buttered or oiled loaf pan and place in the preheated oven.

Bake for one hour.

MEAT AND MEAT SUBSTITUTES

The question here is to get the maximum of flavor and nutrition out of each piece of meat via natural means. This is easy enough when broiling a tender steak, but what do you do with one of the tough hunks? The answer is: you tenderize it—using *natural* aids. Some natural tenderizers are listed below:

Time: A stew cooked for long hours over a low fire can result in meat as tender and succulent as filet mignon.

Wine: The addition of wine to a pot roast or a stew speeds the tenderizing process. Overnight marinades are also often wine-based.

Vermouth: It gives the same effect as wine, with a subtly different taste. And by the way, all alcohol will have evaporated by the time you get around to eating the meat, so you needn't be afraid to serve it even to children.

Cognac: This has a similar effect, but is far more expensive, of course.

Vinegar: Vinegar is an excellent tenderizer, with yet another flavor to impart.

Tea: Yes, good old tea! It also adds a rich brown color to your pot roast gravy or stew liquid.

Incidentally, if you have simmered meat in liquid, remember that the liquid will have received much of the meat's nourishing values. This liquid is what the cookbooks refer to as "stock." *Never* discard it, but integrate it with the dish or use it as a base for another one. The liquid should not be kept for long before using, as it soon loses its freshness.

Those who eschew the eating of meat have beans and nuts and their own specialized diets and cookbooks to guide them.

MILK

It has always been recognized that milk and milk products are essential to health. One of the most famous of milk products is yogurt, and it certainly does seem that every time a news item appears bearing the details of the world's oldest inhabitant (usually found in a place like Bessarabia), it turns out his diet has contained lashings of yogurt.

Whether yogurt alone is responsible for longevity is debatable, but it certainly is good for your health. It is also cheap and easy to make. No special equipment is necessary either, no matter what the advertisements tell you.

YOGURT
4 cups milk
1 cup powdered milk
1 container of plain yogurt (about 1 cup)

Put all the ingredients in an enamel-lined pan and stir them together, over very low heat, with a wooden spoon or spatula. (It must be a *wooden* instrument; metal is not good for milk products.)

Heat to body temperature—that is, to where the mixture feels the same as the temperature of your finger, or slightly cooler.

Remove from the fire at once and let it sit, covered, in a warmish place—say, on a water heater or in the oven with *only* the pilot light on and the door slightly open.

It should take about three hours to form, but I have known it to take as long as twelve. Just peep at it every so often. At first, a few small "islands" of solid stuff may show on the surface, little dots about the size of the nail on your little finger, or smaller. And then, suddenly, there it is—solid yogurt from pan edge to pan edge. Refrigerate it immediately, and it will keep for several days, even a week—but chances are you'll have eaten it all up long before that.

To start a new batch, just save the last cupful of your yogurt and use it instead of a commercial cupful. I've kept this going for five or six batches, and then the strain of yogurt bacillus seems to grow weak or something. At that point, start again from scratch with a plain yogurt bought at the store.

For recipes calling for either buttermilk or sour cream, you'll find the results of the mixtures below do splendidly as stand-ins.

BUTTERMILK
Add 1 tablespoon fresh lemon juice per cup of regular milk.

SOUR CREAM
You can use sweet cream or, failing that, evaporated milk or irradiated milk. To each cup, you add either 1 tablespoon of fresh lemon juice or 1 tablespoon of vinegar. (I'd avoid wine vinegar if I had the choice, but in an emergency, go ahead.)

VEGETABLES AND FRUIT
The term "organic" has been much abused of late, but, no two ways about it, fruit and vegetables grown in correctly balanced, natural soil, taste infinitely better than their counterparts that have been forced, picked green, artificially ripened, or chemically boosted.

You can test this for yourself by comparing the flavor of, say, a field tomato bought at a farmland roadside store in the fall, to the spongy, pale round tomato that appears on the supermarket shelf all year round.

Mammoth strawberries out of season *look* simply stupendous, but do they taste it? If you put lots of sugar and cream on them you can ooh! and ahh! yourself into believing that the taste is great, but if you consider that strawberry (unbiased by the outrageous price you paid for it), you'll find it's a different story.

So one guiding rule is: *buy seasonal fruits in season*. They taste their best at this time; they're also at their cheapest. This is yet another example of the ecologically sound being economically beneficial.

Some seasonal vegetables, of course, are normally available for so much of the year that they appear to be year-round staples.

Actually, the vastness of this country allows for many different growing regions, with as many different times of harvest.

But because of packing and transportation and the distances involved, most fruit is picked on the green side. When you buy it—unless you are buying directly from a local grower—chances are it is still not at its peak point of ripeness. The thing to do, therefore, is to keep most fruit *outside* the refrigerator. Check it automatically every day and as it reaches full ripeness, put it in the refrigerator if you want to keep it, or if you like your fruit cold.

Melons will always benefit from a couple of days' waiting before being chilled. A melon should have a faint melon smell to be adjudged ripe enough to eat. Avocados are also in line for the waiting treatment. They should be soft to the touch at the neck end. I've had some sit on a sunny kitchen window sill for a week before they hit their stride—but then, after some hours in the refrigerator, they were truly delicious. Peaches are another fruit that bear a little home-maturing.

Keep bananas out, however, if you want them to ripen fast, but if you want to hold them back, just stash them on the refrigerator shelf. They take far longer to ripen where it's cool and dark (and no, it *won't* ruin them).

Vegetables are another matter: they do get put into the refrigerator when you get them home. When you wash them for use, do so quickly; soaking vegetables for long periods of time can drain off nutrients.

Have you any idea how many vegetables can be eaten raw? And how much more nutritious they are in that state? Salads with plenty of raw vegetables are excellent not only for internal health, but for the teeth and gums as well. Try things like spinach, string beans, cauliflower, cabbage, carrots, broccoli, and all kinds of greens—cut, torn, or shredded and added to more conventional salad makings.

When you use cucumbers, slice them skin and all—but scrub them well first, preferably with a vegetable brush, since they are often waxed for display purposes. One cannot help reflecting that we would all be better off healthwise if there were a lot less concern about display and a lot more about basic value.

It seems extraordinary to have to emphasize this point, but it appears necessary to do so: fruit and vegetables should be judged by *taste*, not appearance. Think of the apples that look sort of crabby and somewhat misshapen outside (usually ones from somebody's back yard), but are crisp to the bite and taste sweet and juicy; then think of the picturesque, shiny red and yellow balloons of apples you got from the store, that tasted like cotton.

In many European countries no housewife would dream of buying fruit that she had not been allowed to taste first. Superficial looks take second place where people really care about what they eat and what they pay for. Unhappily, American packaging and marketing of fruit is not conducive to a free taste. Which brings us back to the principle of *caveat emptor*.

According to most nutrition experts, in order to preserve the best in vegetables, almost any cooking method is better than boiling. One of the best ways is to steam vegetables. A rack holds the vegetable above the small quantity of water necessary and the steam that rises from it does the necessary cooking. Purists point out that even this minimal amount of water will have absorbed some of the vegetables' nutrients, so if you have a soup pot going, or a stew, add this liquid to it and gain full nourishment.

Attention to such details as these can become a habit that is automatic. It's a habit that will benefit you and your family and ensure that no food is wasted—in the real sense of the term.

6.   Human Energy

It is a paradox today that never before have so many pep pills and sleeping pills been sold throughout the country—and never before have so many people complained of flagging energies or insomnia.

Granted, there may be times when medico-chemical aid is necessary. But most of the time, a well-balanced form of life and nutrition will give you all the sleep and energy you require. For those times when extra aid is needed, the suggestions that follow will be of great help.

To boost your energy, you must first try to define your type of fatigue. If, for example, you have been waking up tired after a full night's sleep, there is something wrong with either your health, or your life style, or your emotional life, and you'd better take a closer look at the underlying problem.

If you wake up just fine, but tend to fold or sag at the knees around 11:00 A.M. a change of breakfast menu (or a mid-morning snack) may prolong your energy. The after-lunch slump or the post-dinner party pooper indicate rather too much food during the meal; stuffing oneself causes somnolence, or at least a dull and logy feeling, hardly conducive to quick movement or enthusiastic energy to tackle chores or pastimes.

FOOD

One means toward more and better energy is: "less food more often." As long as the foodstuffs chosen are nutritionally sensible, these smaller, more frequent meals and snacks will avoid the lows caused by both too empty and too full a stomach.

A good breakfast energy-giver and sustainer is Muesli. (The recipe is given on page 64.) Muesli is nutritious, delicious, and just about the best all-round day-starter. Once converted to Muesli, few people ever go back to the oversweetened, blah-tasting cereals that were once their breakfast staple.

Other breakfast possibilities when there's an active, crowded day ahead are a small steak (after all, no one thinks twice about bacon for breakfast), or a slice of broiled or pan-fried liver, or a bowl of oatmeal sweetened with honey.

Honey is one of the energy-giving greats. A spoonful of it at any time that the spirit is willing but the energy weak will do much to restore the ability to keep on going. A small glass of milk with some honey in it is another quick pick-me-up favorite.

Interestingly enough, this energy-snack recipe is also recommended as a before-bed snack for insomniacs. A chemical balance is needed within the body to allow it to achieve its required state—whether that state be wakefulness or sleep. Honey helps gear your body to the required action: milk helps prolong the effect.

A different variety of energy booster and pick-me-up is a tablespoon of brewer's yeast dissolved in a glass of fruit juice, or a cup of consommé if you prefer a savory flavor. Or you can opt for fruit juice, pure and simple; the fructose within it is the energizing agent. But let "pure" be the operative word, by which is meant "fresh." Canned and frozen juice have good qualities, but freshly obtained juice, from the ripe fruit itself, is superior in all aspects.

A whipped concoction of a glassful of port or Bordeaux wine, one egg yolk, and either sugar or honey to taste, was a great Victorian-era favorite for exhaustion, and it is just as valid today for those who like its flavor. (Honey is nutritionally preferable to sugar.) Also used as a convalescent food, this drink can certainly perk up flagging spirits.

Leave out the wine, and you get another old-world favorite: the beaten richness of egg-yolk and honey, taken straight.

A handful of raisins, well-chewed, can be a quick boost to sagging vigor at a low point in the day. For some people, three or four almonds, also well-chewed, will do the trick, yet this effect may be more psychological than nutritional.

The recipe that follows might well be termed the all-purpose energy snack. Actually, it's more than a snack; it can be breakfast or lunch on a busy day, when time is at a premium and heavy foods must be avoided.

BLENDED BREAKFAST/LIQUID LUNCH
juice of 1 orange
                    (or juice of 1 grapefruit)
juice of 1 lemon
1 whole egg
1 teaspoon brewer's yeast
1 glass milk
honey to taste (at least 1 teaspoon)

If you have a blender, fine and dandy; if you haven't, put all the ingredients except the egg into a jar with a screw-cap top. Shake well. Then, in a separate container, beat the egg. Add beaten egg to the mixture in the jar. Cover tightly again and shake well.

With a blender, you just drop all the ingredients in together, give it a good whizz around, and that's it.

Quick and easy, nourishing and lasting, this Blended Bombshell will keep you going for hours.

PACING

Sometimes it is not added food that we need to keep up our energies, but different pacing, that is, a change in our daily schedules. To sit down if one has been standing, to stand up and walk around if one has been sitting—these are physically beneficial changes. No one is asking the desk-sitter to run a marathon or the salesgirl to lie down under her counter (though she may feel like collapsing there every so often, if she doesn't take that all-important break when she needs it). Nonetheless, a change of position, pace, and attitude every now and then does much to revive energy, and defeat muscular cramping and mental fatigue due to tension. To break the set pace is to rearrange one's energy impulses into more positive patterns.

The long-established coffee break is an example of this, although tea would probably be a better beverage from the restorative point of view.

Since few people work lying flat on the floor, this is probably the most beneficial alternative for a break. Agreed that not many workers are likely to have a patch of carpeted floor handy on which they can stretch out—however, it is suggested that sedentary workers take their coffee breaks standing (there's no law that says you *have* to drink sitting down), and have a little stroll around between sitting spells. Those whose day is spent mostly on the feet might be able to take their breaks *with their feet up:* that is, with the behind on one chair and the ankles and feet up on another. Or, sitting lengthwise along a bench. Shoes off, to make the whole attitude more restful.

But, if you can manage to stretch out (if you work at home, or in a private, carpeted office), get down on the floor. Marble floors are not recommended for winter, nor are wooden ones for that matter—choose a spot where there's carpet or rug, or failing that, spread out a thick bath towel. (Even the firmest of beds gives to a certain degree under pressure, and you want a firm, hard surface underneath you.)

Now, the whole point of getting flat on the floor is to let yourself go as limp as possible. However, to do this right off the bat is not always as simple as it sounds. You may find that whereas you've been able to let your arms and legs feel all loose and floppy, there is an unmistakeable knot of stiff tension in the small of your back. What's more, your neck is knotted and stiff.

Therefore, the trick is to stretch out—and then *deliberately* tense yourself up all over. Tighten *everything,* even your fists. Clench up your toes and your jaw. Squeeze your lips together, your eyes.

And then suddenly—let go. The result should be the total relaxation you were seeking in the first place. Just a very few minutes of this, then a slow sitting up and a good stretch or two should revitalize you and help you return to your duties with renewed energy and a clearer outlook.

SLEEP

The two main facts about sleep that should be kept in mind are that (1) sleep is an absolutely normal function, and (2) *everybody* falls asleep eventually.

All those stories about "I can *never* sleep" or "I haven't slept a wink in *days*" are simply not true. Above all, insomnia should be considered as a symptom rather than a disease in itself. To cure it, the cause must be found, and when the causative factor is removed, sleep will come naturally again.

Most people's insomnia is not so much a question of not sleeping at all, but of not sleeping *easily.* And just about the worst thing the insomniac can do is worry about it. It is far, far better just to let it take its course. If you can't sleep, don't lie there getting all upset about it; switch on the light and do something. Get up again, if that appeals to you. Read. Clean out a closet. Work on your stamp collection. If there are other people in the house, consideration for them prevents the possibility of noisy activity, but how about writing that letter (or those letters) you've been meaning to do for so long? Or tackling some task you've been trying to avoid? Or sitting down to have a good long think about *why* you have insomnia. Or perhaps you already know the cause (you have present worries or an emotional hang-up). If you do, just put the wakeful time to constructive use; it's not the wakefulness that is harmful, but the *worrying* about it that drags one down.

When there is a medical reason for insomnia (pain, disease, etc.), it is only a doctor who can cope with aiding the patient, and no "home cure" should ever be attempted. Such cases are proportionately rare in the great ranks of the restless nonsleepers, and nothing in this chapter is to be applied to them. But for the average, healthy insomniac (and, individual as we like to think our cases are, they still have underlying facets in common, and accepting this fact is a first step toward cure), constructive use of the nonsleeping time can be of enormous help.

Then, when the first signs of peripheral drowsiness appear, it's a good idea to have a warm and soothing drink and tuck down in bed once more. As mentioned earlier, milk sweetened with honey is a good sleep aid—and it is preferable to drink it warm.

Thyme tea is also recommended. Pour a cupful of boiling water over a tablespoon of thyme. Let it steep for five minutes, then strain, sweeten with honey, and drink while still warm.

Camomile tea is another long-time favorite, and is now available in tea bags in many stores. Peppermint is also used in this manner and a brew made of aniseed (same method as for thyme, except you use a teaspoonful of the seeds instead) has its devoted fans, too.

It is perhaps comforting to realize that sleeping too much can be as enervating as sleeping too little. For the average adult, who needs from seven to nine hours of sleep per 24, a sleep period of over ten hours can leave him or her feeling exhausted and fuzzy-minded. (*Not*, of course, if the long sleep takes place after an over-long period of wakefulness and activity, for then the sleeper is compensating for the excessive energy drain to the system. But if a day of normal activity precedes the sleep, chances are high that the subject will wake befuddled and "tired.")

The goal to aim for, of course, is good balance—for when energy and sleep are in perfect relation to each other, a human being's potential for life and its enjoyment is at full value.

7. Specific Foods for Special Needs

I have already pointed out that natural good health is best brought about by natural good foodstuffs. However, there are times when special situations and physical conditions call for certain foods.

The special circumstances discussed in this chapter are by no means the only ones, nor are the suggested dietary aids the only solutions. They are, nonetheless, among those most frequently met with, and the first one is probably the most often discussed.

SLIMMING

There are so many detailed weight-loss diets available in print, that to include a selection here seems pointless, so let's stick to miscellaneous tips to help the dieter along on whatever regime has been selected.

(1) While on a diet, keep busy. If you're involved in work, hobbies, volunteer activities, or a special project, you will have little inclination and even less time to think about food.

(2) Unless the diet specifically forbids it, remember to drink a full glass of water first thing in the morning and before each meal. It helps cleanse your insides—and it helps fill you up.

(3) Don't talk about your diet. Just do it. It is, after all, of prime importance to you, but not to the world at large. The exception is if you are in a group-therapy situation.

(4) Crash diets are seldom advisable, and *never* for those who must lose a great many pounds. Weight should be lost and kept off by a carefully diminished food intake maintained at a constant level. Well-balanced diets are essential for health; to live on nothing but carrots and papaya juice, or eggs and milk, for more than a very few days at a time is deliberately to invite trouble.

However, if all you need to shed is three or four pounds and you're in good general health, then a crash diet may be permissible. (Remember you should never go on a diet of any kind without your doctor's permission.)

Every year brings new fashions in crash diets. Bananas and milk—and nothing else for three days—was a big hit a number of years ago. Recently, pineapple, and only pineapple for 24 hours was the simple (and simple-minded) rule.

The trouble with crash diets is that they are unbalanced in their nutritional content and to starve basic needs in matters of cellular maintenance is not at all wise. The weight loss will be there—but for how long and at what price? The haggard look of overzealous or unbalanced dieting is hardly the desired goal. So use the crash diet only if you want to drop a mere pound or two, *or* if you want to launch a long-term diet and your doctor confirms such a vigorous start will not hurt you.

(5) In that case, make the smash start a healthful one: a day of nothing but vegetable juices and fruit juices, if you are not very active; cooked vegetables and fruit juices if you need some solids to keep you going.

(6) The dieter with a sweet tooth has an extra burden. To lessen it, oranges are the answer. The idea is to eat an orange, section by section, *slowly*. It reduces the craving for sweets.

CONSTIPATION

This is sometimes brought on by dieting, or by foolish dietary habits. It can also be caused by a sluggish pace of life or, for some people, by certain medications. (I have known of people who clutched right up on one aspirin!)

The "laxative habit"—one of those memorable phrases coined by the advertising world—is not at all a good idea. Some laxatives rob the system of vital substances, while others make the muscles and nerves plain lazy. Laziness can breed atrophy, and atrophy means big trouble. It's just not worth getting to the state where you have to rely on laxatives to make your body function— especially since the natural aids are so easy to prepare and take.

(1) Prunes. Yes, prunes are still high favorites in the natural aid department. Try cooking them in weak tea, and adding a squeeze of lemon, for greatly improved flavor.

(2) Yogurt. This all-around health food has a direct and beneficial effect on the intestinal flora—those organisms essential to our inner well-being. Some yogurt on a daily basis is an excellent idea; it does not need to be a huge plateful, either. A half cup per day will do.

(3) Apples. If raw, they must be well-chewed; if cooked, stewed is best. No matter what their form, the old adage has its roots in truth: an apple a day will certainly do much to keep the doctor away and constipation at bay.

(4) Water. And lots of it. A glass of water first thing in the morning is another good all-around habit. Sipping now and then doesn't count: it must be a full quantity drunk down steadily. (Avoid gulping anything; you'll be swallowing air, too, which will only cause discomfort or a grandiose belch.)

The point of a full glass of water into an empty stomach is to get as much of the water as possible to work its way through the intestines. Sipping causes it to be siphoned off by the kidneys, and it is the intestines that need the water cure when you're battling constipation.

So aim for at least a quart of water a day and make one glass a before-breakfast must. Try to drink the rest on an empty stomach, too—that is, always drink it *before* meals.

(5) Black coffee. If you follow your early morning glass of water with a cup of hot black coffee, you'll probably find your system reacts just as you wanted it to.

(6) Walking. A walk around the block is better than no walk at all, so even if it's a short one, make it a daily habit. Taken after dinner, it'll help you sleep better too. The longer the walk, the more beneficial to your system.

WATER RETENTION

Only a medical doctor can prescribe diuretic pills and a specifically diuretic diet for anyone with real water-retention problems. There are many people, however, who suffer mild bouts of this trouble from time to time—some women in the few days preceding menstruation, for example, may experience swollen feet and puffy ankles, saggy-baggy eyelids, and similar nuisances—to say nothing of a general bloated feeling. The following gambits will lessen the effect and its attendant discomforts considerably; again, this is supposing that the condition is not serious enough to warrant a visit to your doctor.

(1) Cut out salt. If you can't bear to cut it out, at least cut it down.

(2) Eat some pineapple (preferably fresh pineapple).

(3) Have a cup of hot coffee *first* thing in the morning, and follow it quickly with two glasses of cold water. Go back to bed and lie down for ten minutes. Then get up to face the day.

The coffee and the water will have geared up the water-elimination system within your body, which should then start functioning properly and get rid of the excess liquid in you.

TIME OF STRESS

Not only what you eat but *how* you eat becomes acutely important during times of stress. Bolting down food when your whole system is tense may well compound your problems; to skip food altogether because tension blocks off appetite is not a good idea either.

People under tension use up energy at a faster rate than usual. Fuel is needed to keep that energy going. Also, such people should not have to spare extra energy to digest heavy foodstuffs or overabundant meals.

Three general rules apply in this situation:

(a) Eat lightly.

(b) Eat slowly.

(c) Eat often.

In general, avoid extremes. Your system has enough to cope with under tension, so don't burden it further. Avoid the too-hot and the too-cold, the too-spicy and the too-rich, too much roughage and too much stimulation.

Milk and milk products, shakes and puddings are all excellent standbys in time of stress. Crackers, peeled fruit, warm vegetable soup—all such foods will keep you going without adding extra stress to the already overloaded system. Honey helps here, too, and tea with milk is usually better than a cup of coffee.

If you feel very tense and are worrying that the tension will prevent your getting to sleep, eat a light and early supper (at least one hour before you go to bed). Make the meal something you have always found soothing: maybe an old childhood favorite. A glass of milk and a peanut butter sandwich; or bread and milk; or a plate of cereal—you know your own favorite. I have a friend who swears by the soothing qualities of a *small* portion of spaghetti cooked *al dente* and served with just a knob of sweet butter.

As the tension lessens, food intake can increase. Above all, remember protein is needed, and energy-giving foods, to rebuild the inner sources depleted by the extra output of energy.

POST-FLU RECUPERATION

Flu, or even a series of winter colds, can leave one feeling debilitated. In the more virulent flu strains, often the period of recuperation far outweighs the illness itself in time and prolonged discomfort. There are physical reasons for this: the body is exhausted. For rebuilding body strength, the recipes in the section after this one are all indicated in the post-flu period, too. However, specifics for post-flu recuperation include:

(1) Lots of mold cheese and yogurt. Not only has the flu knocked your body for a loop, but the antibiotics you took to knock out the flu bug also knocked out some of that intestinal flora. The miracle drugs can be singularly undiscriminating; they wage war against a full range of micro-organisms, good and bad alike. Yogurt and mold cheese will help your system replenish its own vital organisms.

(2) Intensify your intake of protein. Meat, fowl, fish, eggs, all cheeses, and egg custards should dominate your meals. Green salads and fresh fruit should also figure in the diet.

(3) Avoid heavy foods, or foods that put a strain on your digestive system.

(4) Avoid alcohol for a while, other than in minimal quantity with meals, such as a glass of red wine with your dinner, if you are partial to that sort of pick-me-up.

(5) Get lots of sleep. Try for an extra hour per night and a midday nap if possible. Avoid getting overtired at all costs, or you risk inviting another virus to hop aboard your weakened body.

RECUPERATIVE FOODS

The road to regained health is paved with special foodstuffs. The following recipes are time-tested: good nourishment, easily digested, enable the body to rebuild its strength, energy, and resources.

Invalids and recuperating patients are usually more easily coaxed with small and varied snacks than with full meals. The exhaustion that results from being ill—akin, in its way, to battle-fatigue—can leave people with little interest in food. Therefore, the dual objective of the recuperative recipe is to tempt the palate as it nourishes the system.

FOOD FOR FEVER

When fever is present, no meat and few solids should be given. Frequent small amounts of fruit juice are recommended, fresh if possible, and served cool or at room temperature but never very cold.

As the fever lifts, and solid food becomes a possibility once more, those best suited are stewed fruit, tender stewed vegetables, oatmeal soup, mashed potatoes, and light sweets such as apple jelly.

OATMEAL SOUP

4 tablespoons oatmeal
2 cups water
pinch of salt
1 egg yolk

Mix the oatmeal with the cold water and the pinch of salt and bring it to simmering point. Cook thus for half an hour.

Remove from fire, put through a fine sieve, and stir in the egg yolk just before serving.

APPLE JELLY

1 pound apples
1 cup water
1 lemon quarter
2 tablespoons sugar

dash of cinnamon

4 envelopes of gelatin, dissolved in water

Core and chop apples. Stew together with water, sugar, lemon section, and cinnamon until soft. Put the mixture through a sieve, add melted gelatin, and pour into a mold. Cool before serving.

QUICK APPLE JELLY

A "quick" adaptation may be made by adding a cupful of the apple mixture to a package of ready-made gelatin dessert. Simply substitute the sieved apple purée for one of the cups of water required by the gelatin mix:

1 package gelatin dessert mix

1 cup boiling water

1 cup apple purée

Add boiling water to the gelatin and mix well. Then add the apple purée. (If the purée is exceptionally thick, an additional ¼ to ½ cup water will prevent the jelly from being too firm.) Cool to set before serving.

Another palatable and strength-building vegetarian food is barley.

BARLEY SOUP

3 tablespoons barley

1 carrot

parsley

pinch of salt

2 cups water

1 egg yolk

Put the barley, carrot, parsley, salt, and water into a pan and simmer for two hours. Pass through a sieve and add the egg yolk before serving.

As more progress is made, and meat becomes viable once more, two excellent ways of reintroducing it are beef tea and veal purée.

BEEF TEA

½ pound chopped lean beef

½ cup cold water

Put the beef and the water into a glass jar. Place the jar in a pan and fill the pan with water, halfway up the glass jar. Cover and simmer for two hours.

Force the contents of the jar through a sieve. Beef tea can be served full-strength by the teaspoonful for body-building purposes, or with hot water added as a cup of warm liquid.

VEAL PURÉE
½ pound veal
butter
bouillon (if needed)
dash of salt
1 egg yolk (optional)

Cut the veal into small cubes and cook with a little butter until well done. Pass it through a sieve, add a little bouillon if necessary, also a dash of salt. An egg yolk can be stirred in before serving.

Body-building snacks to be served any time include drinks and light sweets. A beater or a blender is handy to have for many of these, but two forks held together with the tines slightly out of alignment will work admirably in the absence of a specific beating tool.

EGGNOG
1 cup milk
1 egg
dash of brandy *or* drop of vanilla essence

Either mix in a blender, or beat well. If alcohol is not advisable, you can use the vanilla essence instead of the brandy.

GRAPE-NOG
½ cup grape juice
1 tablespoon lemon juice
1 tablespoon honey
1 egg

Beat all the ingredients together until smooth (and incidentally, if the grape juice is fresh, the nutritional value is that much higher. To make fresh grape juice, put grapes in blender, give them a whizz around, and strain.)

WINE FLIP
1 cup white wine (or 1 cup apple juice)
1 egg
2 egg yolks
4 tablespoons sugar (or, preferably, honey)
Mix all the ingredients together, then beat the mixture in a double boiler until thick.

SWEET OMELETTE
5 tablespoons sugar
5 egg yolks
5 egg whites (beaten stiff)
8 tablespoons sifted flour
3 tablespoons butter
jam, jelly, or marmalade
Beat the sugar and the egg yolks together. Add flour, still beating, then fold the mixture lightly into the beaten egg whites.

Melt butter in pan and allow to get very hot. Pour in egg mixture: cook on one side, then place in hot oven to finish. (It will cook very quickly.) Remove from oven, spread jam, jelly, or marmalade in the center, fold omelette over once, and serve.

Although nothing can replace a sieve for preparing foods for early convalescence, the later stages can take more roughage, and a blender is useful here. A vegetable drink with body-building properties is simple to make when the liquefying is done mechanically.

MIDMORNING BOOSTER
equal amounts of:
chopped carrots
chopped celery
spinach leaves
1 teaspoon parsley

Drop all ingredients into blender and liquefy. Drink cool but not ice cold.

By this time the patient is probably up and about. Fortified milk drinks can still be coaxed in: varieties are endless, but the following is excellent because it incorporates building and cleansing properties.

BANANA SHAKE
1 cup milk
½ cup yogurt
1 small banana (or ½ large one)
Whip together through blender and serve.

THE GRANDDADDY DIET

The truth is, of course, that the basis for a healthy and enjoyable old age is laid down during all the years that precede it. Reach the golden years in good health, lively spirits, and with an interested outlook, and they will be golden indeed.

To maintain these qualities, a few simple rules and an intelligent approach to food go a long way. Anyone who has a member of the older generation in the household will find it perfectly simple to incorporate the pointers that follow into the general food-preparing routines. Those oldsters who live on their own will discover that following these rules will add to their general well-being.

GENERAL RULES

1. If dentures are worn, they should be fitted and adjusted until they are really comfortable. No making do, here.

2. Food should be properly and carefully chewed. It should never be eaten in a hurry. Liquids should be sipped, never gulped. Above all, food should be enjoyed, not endured.

3. Five small meals a day are better than three large ones: breakfast, midmorning snack, lunch, midafternoon tea, and dinner. A bedtime snack is a good idea if enjoyed, and if the daytime snacks have been kept light.

4. Dietary balance should emphasize fruit and vegetables and proteins. These are the youth keepers and energy givers.

5. If honey can be substituted for sugar, do so. (It usually can: all that is needed is a pot of honey and a firm will.)

6. Avoid all soft drinks and sugar substitutes. As a general pick-me-up and health toner, mix a half tablespoon of brewer's yeast in a half cup of water. This can be taken three times daily. It aids both the health and the memory.

7. Eat as many raw salads, vegetables, and fruits as possible. Get a blender and/or a grater to deal with those items that require presoftening to accommodate personal capabilities. Red cabbage, for example, chopped or shredded and eaten raw in salad form, contains valuable vitamin C and is easier on the digestive system raw than when it is cooked.

8. Tone down the intake of *white* sugar (remember honey), *white* flour, and *white* starches such as spaghetti, macaroni, and *white* rice. In these cases, *white* is not pure but devoid of vitamins.

9. A glass of wine or beer with meals can be enjoyable, relaxing, a digestive aid, and nutritive. Stronger forms of alcohol are usually only temporary boosters and lack real beneficial substance. However, for the oldster who suddenly feels depressed and poorly, a shot of brandy can be quite a lifesaver (assuming that there is no medical reason why alcohol should not be taken in small quantities).

10. Whole grains and whole meal flour should always form a steady part of the diet. They give full value of minerals, proteins, and vitamins, and provide roughage which wards off constipation, frequently a problem of the less active years. (That's another reason honey should be eaten: it is a natural and gentle aid to the intestinal system.)

Whole rice, barley, buckwheat, and whole meal flour are all in the whole grain category. Oatmeal is also excellent, and a long-favored breakfast food is often made with it, although Muesli can also be made with other forms of grain.

MUESLI
(Exact quantities are not critical. The measurements given below would serve two people.)

2 tablespoons oatmeal or other grain, uncooked
½ cup water
Leave these two ingredients to soak overnight. Next morning for breakfast you add:
2 apples, chopped or grated
¼ to ½ cup nuts, grated (almonds, walnuts, hazelnuts)
½ cup milk
squeeze of lemon juice
raisins or sultanas (optional)
Mix all ingredients and serve.

Muesli is just about the best breakfast food there is. Its use should certainly not be restricted to the diet of the elderly. Muesli makes the perfect family breakfast, ensuring that everyone, from the youngest to the oldest, has a good nutritional start for the day.

8. Nature's Tranquilizers

Sometimes outside pressures and inner tensions rise well above the level of mere discomfort. Even for people who are naturally calm, or for those who appear calm on the surface, sometimes the going gets rough. It is then that we begin to be concerned about the wear and tear upon our "nerves" and the subsequent reactions.

It is true that there is a wide range of little pills with which we can "tranquilize"—in other words, deaden—our nerves. These pills are dispensed and sold in incredible quantity. Yet one is hardly aware of a population that is growing more and more serene.

Certain chemical tranquilizers have been found to have reverse effects on small children; that is, the so-called tranquilizer has caused a child to go into a hyperactive state of mind and body. *No tranquilizer should ever be given to a child unless specifically prescribed by a doctor.* Parents who indiscriminately feed such pills to their children are little less than criminal.

Anyone who still believes that old chestnut about the strain of contemporary life should consider what the strain must have been

like in the plague-ridden, witch-hunting Middle Ages, where if
Bubonic didn't get you, the Inquisition probably did. Or, when
Attila, Genghis, *et al.* roared over whole continents. Or during
times of famines and fevers, riots and revolutions. Or in the days
of the pioneers in the West.

No, the times and tides of mankind have *never* been tranquil—
but man can, each in his own way, do much within natural bounds
to reinforce his own capacity for achieving serenity in a troubled
world.

The inner tranquility built on inner resources represents far
greater eventual strength than the emotional anaesthesia provided
by a pill. There are times, of course, when medication is a great
aid—but these times should be exceptional occasions that call for
exceptional measures. To treat tranquilizers like everyday candy is
only to diminish one's true resources.

Nervous tension can be separated into two main categories. The
first is the short-term acute kind. Stage fright, exam funk, the
pre-speech nerves of the after-dinner speaker all come into this
category, as do temper fits and tears. The second is a chronic, or
long-term category. Here, tension is caused by a prolonged
situation of high stress. Emotional and physical tiredness—indeed,
even exhaustion—come into the picture here.

There are natural aids that can help in both categories. As they
help the immediate situation, they also help build and reinforce
the inner strength and resources for the future. They build
self-reliance rather than *pill*-reliance.

ACUTE TENSION

The one weapon to use against tension, that is always handy no
matter where you are or what the circumstances, is your own
breath. When nerves clutch up, breathe in slowly; hold your
breath. Breathe out slowly; hold your breath. Do this five or six
times, doing the breathing part more and more slowly and holding
your breath a bit longer each time.

The best breathing nerve control is the Belly Dance Breath. If
you're not in public, start it the moment nerves jangle. (If you are
in public—well, I guess it depends on your public . . .)

(1) Breathe in deeply, blowing your stomach out like a balloon.

(2) Hold your breath, and transfer all the breath inside you upwards by expanding your chest and pulling in your stomach.

(3) Still holding your breath, reverse the movement and blow your stomach into a balloon again.

(It sounds more difficult than it is; you'll get the swing of it first time you try.)

(4) Repeat the in-and-out stomach movement four or five times.

(5) Exhale *slowly,* letting breath out only through your nose.

If you do this three or four times, you'll find the shaky nervousness will disappear.

Sometimes what hits are nervous palpitations. These are both unpleasant and uncomfortable. Should they occur, close your eyes and press your hands gently against your eyelids for a few minutes. The fluttering feeling will ease and go. If you wish, you can then go into the slow breathing routine, but it probably won't be necessary.

Jangled nerves, both of the immediate and the long-term variety, often respond favorably to a walk, the longer the better. Walking is especially good when nervous tension is triggered by anger; healthy circulation enables the body to balance its chemistry again. Sudden emotion—anger, fear, fright, etc.—causes quick, high increases in certain body substances (among them, adrenaline) which walking helps bring to a normal level.

Brisk walks serve best for acute tension; gentle, meandering rambles are often better suited to those suffering from long-term nervous states. The terrain covered also plays its part, and only the individual can decide what is best. For some, a prolonged stroll along a sandy beach is the most calming thing in the world. (The proximity of the sea has much to do with this; water often plays a tranquilizing role. It has also been established that the salt in the air has a beneficial effect on some people's systems.) To others, sand is anathema, and for them a quiet patch of woods is the ideal place for a ramble. They might prefer a river or a lake—perhaps a pond. Just watching a body of water soothes a great many. When it is water in motion (a river, a waterfall, the sea, a brook) the sounds made by its currents and splashing, also play their tranquilizing part.

As for indoor soothers, baths have, from time immemorial, been found to calm the body and steady the spirit, and their worth is as valid and applicable today as it ever was.

BATHS

Running Bath: To gauge the temperature of this bath, use a kitchen thermometer if you have one, for the ideal is to keep the water at 100˚F. Fill up the tub, then open the drain slightly, but keep the water running from the faucet.

Thus a constant stream of 100˚ water enters the tub as an equal flow leaves via the drain. Climb in, wedge a pillow or a rolled-up towel behind your head, and immerse yourself in the water. Stay in there for a good half hour, longer if you feel like it. No exertion, no washing or scrubbing: all you need do is lie there and let yourself go limp in the ever-changing, constant-temperature water. By all means wiggle your toes or splash about if you feel so inclined, but if you don't, just lie back and let the moving, splashing water do the rest.

Post Crying Jag Shower: Whenever nervous tension has exploded into tears, or there has been an emotional crying jag, the answer to both nervous stress and the swollen face is a shower. I mean a very long shower; it can be hot, warm, or cold. The important thing is that the water should really pound down on you. Turn it on full force. Then stay under it, even if you are still crying, until you begin to feel its beneficial effects.

There are multiple effects to be gained by the method. The force of the water acts both physically and psychologically. There is also the sound of the water which plays its part.

Flower Baths: This method is used in clinics that specialize in the treatment of nervous exhaustion by natural means. These are sometimes known as "health cures" and they consist of specialized diets combined with exercises and certain forms of hydrotherapy.

Not all these methods can be reproduced at home because of the equipment that is sometimes necessary. However, these calming flower baths can be reasonably imitated.

Actually, the ideal equipment to use is the lawn sprinkler! So if it is summertime, and you have a lawn or a yard that you can soak, get into a swimsuit, turn on the sprinkler and lie where its fine spray sprinkles you lightly but consistently for several hours.

Failing a lawn sprinkler and the heat of midsummer, you can achieve much the same effect with a shower head and your bathtub. Adjust the shower nozzle to the finest spray possible. If your shower is nonadjustable, an inexpensive dime-store attachment will work just as well.

Turn the water on and let it run warm; lie in the tub under the spray but do not allow water to collect in the tub itself. The beneficial effect in this method is caused by gentle but constant droplets or jets of water landing on the body's surface, and this must not be shielded or interrupted by water accumulation in the tub.

Restimulation Routine: There are times when tension has exhausted one, and yet further duties or activities must be faced before the end of the day. For example, after a day of frustration or private unhappiness or similar exhausting tensions, you may face a formal gathering of some kind during the evening.

The thing to do in this case is to take a hot bath, lie in it for ten minutes or less, then drain off the water and stand under a lukewarm to cold shower. The bath will help ease some of the accumulated tension and the shower will aid the restimulation of the energies that will be needed to get through the required niceties of the evening.

Herbal Baths: Although herb baths are pleasant at any time, there are several that are specifically appropriate for times of emotional stress. To make them, the same methods are used as those described later in this book. Probably the easiest way is to put the herb in a muslin square, tie it up like a hobo pack, and toss it into the bath as the water runs in, allowing it to steep for at least ten minutes.

Herbs that are soothing to the nervous system are camomile, valerian, rosemary, and lavender. Also highly recommended are pine needles; pick them fresh from the tree, wrap them in their hobo bag and use them just as you would use the herb bath bags.

OTHER METHODS

There are many substances—including some of the herbs used in the herb baths—that help calm jangled nerves when used internally. Chewing an apple is often of immediate aid. Not only does the action of deliberate chewing help channel some of the overwrought energy, but the nutritional quality of the apple itself will help rebalance the body chemistry.

Camomile tea is one of the oldest nerve-calming teas known to herb enthusiasts. In many countries anyone suffering from emotional stress is taken off ordinary tea and coffee at once and told to drink either camomile or verbena tea instead. Milk may be added to either one, and should sweetening be desired, honey is suggested. Another calming drink is warm milk with honey.

Music can have tremendously calming effects on some people, but it should not be regarded as an all-around panacea for everybody. There are some people whose nervous and emotional structure will react most adversely to the sound of music; for them silence is golden.

In a general sense, horizontal lines are calming, whereas vertical ones produce stress. Consider the soothing sense that a lake or an open field can give us versus the energizing (and sometimes exhausting) stress generated by a city of skyscrapers. In their own subtle way, the vertical lines of tall buildings add to the stress of life in a city. By contrast, the purposely horizontal construction of a Japanese garden makes it one of the most tranquil sights in the world.

Following on this theme, and adding to it the fact that gentle motions can also be soothing, watching fish swim back and forth in an aquarium has often been cited as a relaxer. At one time it was suggested that aquariums be installed in doctors' and dentists' waiting rooms, thus giving the anxiously awaiting patients something soothing to watch.

Despite the stress quotient of vertical lines, their impact is totally altered when combined with slow motion. I am talking of the effect of watching snow fall; its fall is vertical, but because of its gentle motion the end effect is soothing and calming to the nerves. This is also enhanced by the fact that snow blankets noise;

our individual reactions to sound are inextricably involved with our nervous and emotional systems. As it is with snow, so it is with rain; in the latter case there is a sound to the fall of rain that blankets out or dulls other, sharper sounds.

Keeping in mind the individuality of each person's emotional makeup, it is always best to try to build emotional strength from within. It is up to each individual to find and choose those offerings within the cycle of nature that best support and fulfill his or her individual needs.

PART THREE

THE INDOOR ENVIRONMENT

9. The Seasons and You

Just how closely we are attuned to nature is clearly demonstrated by our reactions to the climate. All of us function in rhythm with the cycle of the seasons and in tune with the balanced order within the changes of weather. There are general effects from these changes, felt by us all—heat in summer, cold in winter, for instance. Then there are more subtle and individual changes, dependent upon varying constitutions and sensitivities.

One does not have to be outdoors in order to be affected by the weather or the seasons, however. The micro-climates of our homes are inevitably affected by the macro-climate outside, no matter how much we may control the air within the house.

It has been established, for example, that hair and nails grow faster in the summertime (hair, by the way, also grows faster when there has been sexual stimulation). Individually, on the other hand, rheumatism sufferers can forecast an oncoming rainfall or snowstorm because of their physical discomfort; they are sensitive to the barometric pressure change that occurs as the weather patterns begin to alter.

Strictly speaking, all forms of man-made or man-caused heating pollute. (Solar heating does not.) It has been said that the first man to light the first fire was, in a sense, the first polluter of the air, for smoke, no matter what its source, is a pollutant. However, there are degrees, and it is a question of coming as close to the correct balance between man's needs and nature's capabilities as is strictly possible.

Within a building, it is better to heat with systems that "glow" heating, rather than those that blow hot air into rooms. The drying effect of hot draughts on people can affect skin, sinus, and general temperament; paintings and furniture can suffer irreparable damage, as well.

As to the actual heating systems themselves—well, despite what the ads say, there is no form of truly "clean" heat. High sulphur-content oil belches pollution into the air; low sulphur-content oil is better, but still not absolutely clean. Gas heating emits minor smoke at the point of burning. The pollution problem with electricity and its apparently "perfect" nonsmoke glow lies at the generating source, for some form of fuel is needed to turn the generators themselves.

There was a time when nuclear plants were believed to be the answer to the heating problem, but recent studies and even more recent public opposition to nuclear plants have proved otherwise. Extensive safeguards are necessary to prevent these plants from overheating river waters, bay areas, and so forth; while it is safe and clean to fry an egg on an electric appliance, the power energizing that fryer may come from a plant that is quite literally boiling the life out of a nearby lake.

We should attempt to realize our full potential within the framework of nature and the seasons, depending on the artificialities of technology only where it enriches or enhances life to a measurable degree. (It is obviously an enrichment of life to live in a heated home during winter.) But to let our own natural capabilities atrophy and to rely on the artificial is unwise and shortsighted, and ultimately, proves unhealthy.

To minimize your dependence on artificial heating systems, recognition rather than manipulation is the all-important factor. To manipulate the climate and surround ourselves with a mass of technological control systems may be important under certain conditions (such as space capsules, where such control is essential to maintenance of life). On a day-to-day basis, however, knowledge of our reactions to natural climatic and weather conditions is of far greater value.

As there are "day" people and "night" people—that is, people whose differing metabolic rates cause them to be most efficient and alert at different times of the day—so there are "spring" and "autumn" people, and "summer" and "winter" people, too.

It is not a question of right or wrong, but one of individual sensitivity and preference. Traditionally, it has been believed that a day filled with sparkling sunshine is "better" than a day of pouring rain. Yet there is no practical reason for this expectation. There are those who function best when the weather is bright and sunny, dry and breezy, but others who prefer dull and overcast, damp and gray days. Recently, it has been realized that many people actually feel calmer and more relaxed on gray rainy days. So there may yet come a time when it will be as socially acceptable to classify oneself as a "rain-lover" as it is today to call oneself a "sun-lover"—an expression that for some reason, bears overtones of virtue!

Be honest with yourself; don't worry about having to build up a false image. Then you will be able to enjoy your favorite seasons to the full, and learn to cope with the others naturally, by preparing for them and thus alleviating the discomforts they bring you.

SPRING AND AUTUMN

These two seasons, dissimilar though they are, can be described together because, in essence, they are seasons of change. One sheds winter's mantle and reveals the growth for the heat of summer ahead; the other harvests and prepares for the coming winter's cold.

Spring, the season of rejuvenation, is the time to shed extra pounds, rev up physical energy after the depleting rigors of winter, clean out the neglected corners, and renew one's attitude to life. As the sap surges, so do ambitions; spring-lovers should take advantage of all the potential energy at their disposal.

For those to whom spring means anxiety and a head cold, the best course of action is a slow but steady program of reenergizing. Such individuals are often slender-framed or downright thin, or with easily depleted energies that have taken a winter beating. Unlike the spring-lovers, who feel their spirits surge at the sight of the first blossom, the anti-spring types have a slow rate of recuperation and they don't have spirits that surge very easily.

Recognition again proves to be the key factor. If a slower pace is necessary, it is better to adapt to it and build up physical stamina carefully rather than force the pace, only to succumb, exhausted, to yet another spring-induced malady.

In autumn the direction is reversed; instead of new growth beginning to shoot up for flowering in the season ahead, we find a harvesting of the fruits to be saved for the winter. Autumn enthusiasts do not need instructions on how to enjoy their favorite season, but autumnphobes might try some gentle exercise to offset their hovering depression.

Cold feet are better warmed by improved circulation than by a heating pad. Again, a good diet helps; spring and autumn are both seasons when diets work best on the system. In either season—depending on your type—you will find that diets for slimming, plumping up, energizing, toning and general shaping-up are easiest to follow and produce their best results.

In spring your diet may be a regime to counteract the aftereffects of prolonged winter fatigue; in autumn, a buildup of energy and strength for the cold ahead may well be in order. As halfway stations, these two seasons give us the chance to recuperate and prepare. If you look around in nature, you'll see it's all part of the larger scheme, too.

SUMMER

If you love summer, you'll find tanning-oil recipes elsewhere in this book (see chapter on skin care) and you don't need much encouragement or guidance about getting the most out of the sun. You may find you seem to soak up energy and health during these months and, as long as you do not exhaust yourself by overdoing an endless round of activities, all the soaked-up energy and stamina will stand you in good stead at the other end of the year.

For those who find summer enervating, or irritating, or plain too hot for comfort, the following guidelines can help ease the season and its attendant ills. Food, attitude, garments, and habits all play their roles.

FOOD

You are probably aware that your liquid intake is greater during the summer. All of us need the extra amount because we perspire more. (I am talking about healthy people; those with physical disorders should talk about dietary balance with their doctors.) But did you know that a slight increase in your salt intake is also frequently advisable? It helps your body retain liquid; in summer heat, this helps regulate the intake-outflow of water through the system.

It is not by coincidence that foods in tropical countries are so often spicy and highly seasoned. It is a climatic adaption of food to environment, a way of best fitting in to the natural order of things. It is also in these climates that the spice-giving plants grow; nature provides appropriate foodstuffs for appropriate regions.

Another good dietary guideline for the hot season: less meat and more vegetables and fruit. Lots of salads and less roasts conveys the idea; lighter meats (fish, poultry) also fit into the scheme of summer menus.

As a rule of thumb, by the way (excluding individual idiosyncrasies), you'll find that slender people tend to be summer fans while plump people tend not to be. The reason is simple: the slender quite literally do not feel the heat as much as the chubby. Extra poundage does make a real burden to carry around in the hot sun, but also, slender folk have automatic cool eating habits (they *like* salads, fruit, small portions of food), whereas the more corpulent have eating habits that are positively heat-provoking (pies and potatoes instead of fruit and salad, chocolate rather than citrus).

ATTITUDE

To beat the heat, the idea is not to fight it (which only tends to make you hotter and even more uncomfortable). Slow down wherever and whenever you can to nature's tempo in midsummer. Stroll, do not stride; murmur instead of shouting. The saying:

Mad dogs and Englishmen
go out in the midday sun

conveys the derision of those native to the tropical lands who watched the discomfort of the English colonizers trying to live as though they were still in a damp, cool climate. To live successfully in an environment, one must learn to accept and live with the inherent qualities of that environment. To fight against it, to try to change it, is to risk missing out on the real benefits to be gained.

Of course, in the hot weather we can stay indoors close to the air-conditioner most of the time. In doing so, however, we are denying ourselves a certain amount of mobility, a certain number of pleasures and activities. We are also weakening our personal resistance by lessening our adaptability.

DRESS

Contrary to popular opinion, stark naked is not necessarily coolest of all. Light covering shields us from the sun and helps absorb and dry off the evaporating perspiration, much of which occurs without our realizing it.

However, perspiration exuded from unclothed skin is less salty than that which comes from covered skin. Therefore, a body clad in a skimpy swimsuit loses less body sodium than the body draped in a long beach robe (all other circumstances, exercise included, being equal). This explains why those Frisbee contestants on the beach may be no more tired at the end of the day than the clothed but lounging spectators.

Tight shoes are a foolish form of self-torture at any time of the year, but in summer they mean the wearer is really storing up trouble for him or herself.

HABITS

Tepid, languid baths are a good start to a hot summer day. Pat yourself dry (no brisk rubdowns at this time of the year) and slip into comfortable, loose-fitting clothes.

Tepid is the best temperature for foot baths, too. You can relieve and revive a pair of aching feet by putting them under the faucet and alternately running tepid and cool water over them. (Several beneficial foot bath recipes are given in the chapter on skin care.)

For middle of the day or evening refresher baths, also stick to the tepid temperature. No matter what you put into the water of your summer bath to make it fresh and pleasant, the temperature should never be extreme.

One last pointer—try sleeping without a pillow. It's good for your spine, good for your neck, and much, much cooler.

A weather occurrence often associated with summer although not exclusive to it is the thunderstorm. Many people feel headaches, depression, general "nervousness," and physical restlessness before the onset of a thunderstorm. Once the rain gushes down the symptoms lift. Some people are quite literally invigorated by that opening clap of thunder and the torrents that follow. Others suffer the prestorm discomfort, but enjoy the downpour afterwards. Being aware of your own reactive pattern helps prevent unnecessary medication, for one thing. An apparently inexplicable headache may seem more tolerable when you've spotted the oncoming storm clouds that are causing it. Knowing that the storm itself will bring relief may help keep a couple of aspirin (or other unnecessary painkiller) out of your system.

WINTER

Winter lovers tend to be hardy and active, possibly endowed with a few more pounds than the summer enthusiasts. These folk enjoy their season and know all the tricks that enable them to get the most out of it.

HABITS

As the trick in summer is to slow down, so the reverse is true in winter: speed up.

Make yourself move. Get the circulation going. Showers start the day: the pounding of the water on the surface of your skin will help the circulation. The brisk towel-rub is winter's drying method, no slouching or lounging around now.

If you come in on a snowy day and your hands and feet feel very chilled, get them under running water, alternately hot and cold. The contrasting temperatures make the capillary veins expand and contract and help restore proper circulation. This sort of treatment prevents the formation of chilblains, one of winter's most uncomfortable annoyances.

DRESS

Did you know that two thin layers will keep you warmer than one thick layer? Air caught between the layers is heated by your body temperature and helps keep you warm by creating a band of insulation between your body and the cold outside. So think in terms of multiple, supple, and soft layers and you'll find you can keep yourself warmer than you thought, without looking like the Michelin tire man.

This system works even on such thin items as stockings. One pair of pantyhose put on on top of another pair is amazingly warm. In wartime, sheets of newspaper have proved this point: tuck a few sheets under a sweater or around your back, and the additional protection is immediately noticeable.

(Another winter use for newspaper: for starting a fire, take a sheet of newspaper, roll it diagonally so as to get the longest roll possible, and then tie the roll into a knot. If it's a full-sized paper, you can roll from top to bottom, but with small sheets, use with the diagonal length. These newspaper knots burn hot, slowly, and well—and can start up a fire, or even provide one if you have no wood around.)

Clog-wearing peoples in northern climes (such as the Dutch) knew what they were doing when they packed their wooden shoes with straw before slipping in their feet. The air trapped between the straw helped hold the body warmth given off by the foot—and after a while each clog was a foot-warming version of a Dutch oven.

There is a pyschological aspect to keeping warm, too. Most of us feel the cold especially keenly in one particular spot. For instance, I have an acquaintance who claims that cold feet are nothing if you've ever suffered from really cold *ears*. So in winter she never goes out without a hat, woolly cap, or warm scarf. This keeps her ears warm—and gives her the feeling of being a lot warmer all over. Check up for yourself on where you feel the cold

most, then take care to keep that sensitive spot protected. You'll
be surprised how much warmer the rest of you automatically feels.

FOOD

Again, the opposite of summer feeding is required—you need
the heat-giving foods in greater quantities than you did during the
keeping-cool routine; winter calls for the heat of soup rather than
the cool of lemonade, hot roast instead of cold cuts, and so on.
Our bodies need the substances that enable us to combat the cold:
it is, after all, the northerly countries that have given us the stews
loaded with starch and fat.

Fat is a good protector against the cold—taken in moderation,
of course. (Think of all the blubber consumed in the Arctic Circle,
not so long ago.) It follows that the coldest days of winter are not
the ideal time to embark on a fat-reduced diet, or any rigorous
diet, for that matter. Chocolate now provides heat and extra
energy.

The wider our range of knowledge and understanding, not only
of the seasons and the climate, but of ourselves within the
constantly changing and renewing cycles, the greater our health,
capabilities, and capacity for enjoyment will be.

10. The Climate Indoors

The atmosphere within your home is as vital to you physically
(and by extension, mentally) as the outdoor climate. As a matter
of fact, it may be of even greater importance, if much of your
time is spent at home.

To one extent or another, we usually regulate the regional
climatic factors by indoor mechanical devices: heaters, air-
conditioners, humidifiers, and artificial light. Naturally, inside we
are also protected from wind, rain, hail, and snow. But there are
subtler factors affecting the indoor climate. Consider the drying
properties of wall-to-wall carpeting. Any extensive stretch of
fabric such as carpeting absorbs a certain portion of the

humidity in the atmosphere—and it may well be that your skin could use the moisture to better advantage than the carpet.

We live and breathe in the environment of our homes for all of our sleeping time and much of our waking time, too. Keep in mind that, statistically, sleep alone occupies a full third of a lifetime. This makes for a big chunk of our lives.

In temperate or cool regions a frequent threat to human health and comfort is too low humidity indoors. This is caused by the heating systems we all love so much. I am not advocating a spartan existence of cool showers, freezing bedrooms, and no heat except around the kitchen stove. But we do need to understand the importance of air moisture for the average human being, and be aware of how quickly it disappears once we start "controlling" the indoor atmosphere by such means as central heating.

It has been said that when the relative humidity drops below 60 to 55 percent, troubles begin. Naturally, some people are more sensitive to the problem than others. Overdryness irritates and eventually damages both the skin surface and the mucous membranes; therefore those who already have some form of extra sensitivity in either of these areas will be the first to suffer.

I would have thought that female vanity alone would have made most women conscious of the hazards of living in dry air. Lots of sun outdoors in summer and an air-dried skin indoors in winter make for some of the deepest and most prominent wrinkles in town. In the last two years, it is true, people have started to become aware of the problem and there are now commercial moisturizers on the market. However, one does not necessarily have to buy machinery to cope with this situation. Moisture can be brought into the atmosphere by other, more natural means.

The house plants mentioned elsewhere will contribute greatly to the atmosphere of your home, just by their own living and transpiration. The fact that you have to keep watering them to ensure *their* good health will also contribute to *yours*.

Another, more direct way of getting moisture into an overdried atmosphere is to keep decorative pots or trays filled with pebbles and water in different parts of the house. Replenish the water as it evaporates. Depending on the heating system in your home, you may be able to place these pots near or on the radiators themselves, thus causing a steady flow of moisture into the rising hot air coming from your sources of heat. The rate at which the water in the pots evaporates may shock you. It certainly reveals how rapidly moisture is used up in the dry indoor atmosphere.

It is not only humans that benefit from a proper humidity balance within the home; furniture and works of art also require a certain amount of moisture if they are to preserve their value and their beauty. Paintings and antique pieces of furniture are particularly vulnerable to overdry air, for it can cause canvas to buckle, paint to slake, and veneer to become brittle and crack or split.

Some form of humidifying process will also keep down that unpleasant product of cold winter living, static electric shock. That's the spark that leaps out to greet you as you reach for a metal doorknob (or another person) after walking quickly across a carpeted surface. It may not be dangerous, but it certainly is irritating and unpleasant, when things you touch "bite" you. A properly humidified room lowers the static electricity and eliminates such shock.

To moisturize a room quickly, soak a bath towel in water, wring it out, and place it over the hot air outlet. Redip the towel every half hour until you feel that the air has attained a comfortable moisture content. If the room has an adjoining bathroom, you are in luck. Run the shower full and hot and let the steam billow through the door into the room. A very few minutes of this treatment solves the problem nicely.

Another factor that should be faced is that many of us tend to overheat our homes. It may be momentarily comfortable, but it can make us more susceptible to such discomforts as winter colds and coughs. Besides it consumes more power and releases more smoke into the atmosphere. A slightly lower temperature and the wearing of a sweater or just slightly heavier clothing can pay off in much better health. After all, hothouse blossoms are never taken into the cold snow, but those of us who lead normal lives cannot afford to let our natural resistance against the cold atrophy, leaving us defenseless.

If an overdry atmosphere is bad for the healthy, it is very much worse for anyone who is sick in bed, or who suffers from a cold or any other ailment that affects the chest or the mucous membranes. It is most important to make sure that a sickroom is kept properly humidified, by any of the means mentioned above (or all of them, if you really have a dryness problem).

For added benefit, boil a pot of water with either mint or eucalyptus leaves, and carry it into the patient's room. If you can keep these sweet-smelling, moist fumes rising by putting the pot right over a heating outlet, so much the better.

The use of eucalyptus leaves in dried arrangements decorating the home may eventually prove to be a health-guard factor. It has been the custom in some parts of the world, when fall begins, to arrange eucalyptus tree shoots in waterless containers (or just lay them flat in a basket) and keep them in a corner of the bedroom and perhaps elsewhere in the house as well. The old wives' theory is that the oil-filled leaves give off a protective something into the air, and that by breathing this within the home one is far less likely to pick up a winter cold. Rumors like this one often prove to have scientific validity; since extractive oil of eucalyptus is used medicinally, a basis for the belief is certainly there.

Smoke can also be a factor in the indoor environment, coming from a fireplace or cigarettes or anything that burns inside the home.

As in so many facets of ecology, balance and proportion are the important things. Sometimes an evaluation must be made and a choice taken.

For example, few things are more cheerful and generally warming to sight, spirit, and body than the leaping flames of an open fireplace. If the room is big and the air otherwise clear, the fact that the fire is both consuming oxygen and giving off smoke is of minor importance to the people sitting around it. But suppose the fireplace is located in a small, cramped room with poor ventilation, in the middle of an industrial city. Under these conditions the fire's consumption of oxygen and emission of smoke may well become less of an inspiration! Where the pollution level is already high, to add yet another burden seems foolish in the extreme, not to mention downright hazardous.

A smoking chimney that doesn't draw properly can often be cleared by a simple method. Wait until the fire has burned down to glowing red embers. Mix dried potato peelings and some cooking salt together (you can use table salt if that's all you have available). About two handfuls each of the peelings and salt should do the trick. Throw them onto the fire, and chances are your chimney problems will stop.

Another kind of smoke to be contended with comes from cigars and cigarettes. At this point I am not discussing the effect upon the systems of the smokers themselves, but upon the indoor climate and therefore on all those who dwell within—smokers and nonsmokers alike.

No matter how one may or may not feel about smoking, the inescapable fact is that tobacco smoke does pollute the air, adding undesirable substances to the air we breathe. (It is only fair to give equal time to marijuana. Again ignoring for the moment the effects upon the individual smoker and the legalities of the situation, the addition of marijuana smoke to the indoor environment is still a form of pollution.) Proof of this has been seen by anyone who has ever washed a pair of curtains from a room in which there has been much smoking. The wash water comes out a dark shade of nicotine brown.

Yet another instance where circumstances must be taken into consideration is the burning of incense; it can create a pleasurable and relaxing atmosphere to those who enjoy it, but they too must think in terms of atmosphere balance. Sound, ecologically balanced living is made up of such mature and careful decisions, in situations where the long-term gain is preferred to the short-term pleasure.

11. Air Fresheners and Deodorizers

I once met a man who was in the insecticide and aerosol bomb business, and a 15-minute conversation with him about his work—during which he talked and I listened—gave me hours' worth of thinking about the subject. The impression I gained was that those sweet-smelling, so-called "deodorizing" air fresheners could just about drop an elephant in its tracks at ten paces. According to this gentleman, it is easier to market these substances as air fresheners than it is to put out-and-out insecticides on sale. I understood that this was somehow linked to marketing regulations; whether this is true or not, all the indications are that the average "air freshener" is a lot stronger chemically than its name and style of advertising would imply.

If you have a cat or a dog in the house, you may have noticed how it runs for cover when you start spraying the air. It's a very wise instinct that prompts the animal to run. Such sprays should never be used on or near any animal (bird, fish or mammal): the average commercial product not only frightens them when it comes hissing out of the can, but its chemicals can cause physical harm.

If you think about it for a moment, you will realize that an aerosol anti-smell substance blankets the smell you are fighting, rather than eliminating it in the true sense. The original odor continues to exist: it is merely that you cannot perceive the smell any more.

In the majority of cases there is no harm in smells. Discomfort or displeasure, yes, sometimes embarrassment, but no active danger. (Please bear in mind that we are talking about household matters; of course there are chemical odors—within the province of industry and science—that can be physically corrosive and highly dangerous.)

It is foolish to be hysterically anti-odor; after all, there are times when an unpleasant smell can be a danger signal—for example, the smell of gas escaping from a burner where the flame has been accidentally extinguished. In such a case, blanketing the smell of gas with something that imitates a gardenia is not only foolish but perilous. What is needed is lots of open windows, plenty of air breezing through the house, and only then a long match to reignite that pilot light.

Unarguably, fresh air—especially early morning fresh air—is one of the greatest home atmosphere cleansers in the world. However, not all of us live in places where such a commodity is readily available. An apartment dweller whose home faces a busy traffic thoroughfare may well object to filling his or her home with the fumes of the morning rush hour. Here, the answer probably lies in opening the windows even earlier or concentrating on such windows as do not face the road. This is not perfectly clean air either, but it may be assumed that the city dweller has come to terms with some sooty air.

For the purposes of simplification, the following anti-smell tips are in two main categories: those useful in the kitchen and those pertaining to the rest of the house.

COOKING SMELLS

ONIONS

Onions, tasty as they are, can present problems in their preparation. It is easiest to keep the smell off your hands by using a knife and fork when peeling and chopping. Another way is to use gloves, although many people find this awkward.

If onions make you cry, hold them in water as you peel them—under the cold water faucet, for example. Or else wear spectacles for the job: sunglasses will do. After this, to get the smell off your hands, rub them with salt and water. Or you may prefer to rub half a lemon over the palms of your hands and each individual finger. Give a final swipe at your nails; droplets of onion juice can lodge under their tips. Yet another method for combating onion smell is mustard, preferably the powdered variety, which is the strongest version. Simply rub some mustard powder or a dollop of prepared mustard all over your hands and then rinse off with cold cream.

Onions on the breath can be gotten rid of by any one of the three following ways:

Chew several coffee grains

Eat a small bunch of parsley

Chomp an apple, peel and all.

BRUSSELS SPROUTS, CABBAGE, CAULIFLOWER

To reduce the pungency of these vegetables' cooking odor, place a crust of bread on top of the vegetables and then cover tightly. (I am assuming that you are either steaming them or boiling them with relatively little water in the pot.)

Incidentally, cauliflower cooks a lot whiter and tastier if you add a dash of milk to the cooking water.

FISH

Don't ask me why, but a piece of apple placed in the pan along with the fish does much to tone down the fishy cooking smell.

The smell of fish on your hands can easily be removed with lemon juice or a lemon half—even a leftover, squeezed-out rind and pulp will serve as a deodorizer.

MISCELLANEOUS

Apple helps with other strong-smelling foods, too, so it is up to the individual cook to try it whenever something with a strong and possibly objectionable smell is being prepared.

Another place in which a chunk of apple can do a good job is inside the refrigerator. Although the new-model "miracle" refrigerators are supposed to do everything for themselves, there are still many thousands of middle-aged models which sometimes need a little help and encouragement. To the refrigerator that may have gotten into the habit of letting tastes and odors swap around rather freely, a chunk of apple can indeed discourage intermingling of the food odors. A lemon half does much the same thing.

A discarded lemon half is always worth holding onto, as it can come in handy at the sink. Both lemon and vinegar have good deodorizing qualities and can eliminate any objectionable smells on your hands.

A bowl of vinegar—preferably the strong white variety—placed next to a pan of frying foods helps keep down both the smoke and the smell of frying. Tips like this are of particular interest to people with small or badly ventilated kitchens. No matter how pleasant the smell of cooking may be, it can get pretty tiresome smelling yesterday's fritters as you are preparing this morning's orange juice.

Many people simply leave a bowl of vinegar permanently by the stove. As the vinegar slowly evaporates, it helps deodorize and clean the atmosphere. Every so often the bowl will need washing out and replenishing so as to keep up its efficacy.

If you want to clean glass bottles or jars thoroughly, hot water mixed with powdered mustard will kill off any lingering smells. Emphasize the water volume rather than the mustard; this is a wash, not a paste.

BEYOND THE KITCHEN

SMOKE

Vinegar is useful not only in the kitchen but in other parts of the house, too. After a party, for example, the smoke-laden atmosphere of the living room can be dispelled far more quickly by placing several bowls of vinegar in different parts of the room.

I know of more than one hostess who actually place the vinegar bowls around the house before the guests arrive. The liquid then begins its work right away, helping to keep the smoke level down during the gathering. If, after the party is over, you clear the ashtrays and either put out the vinegar or leave it out, you can retire knowing you will not have to face a tobacco-reeking room the next morning.

Ammonia works in this same capacity and, since it is stronger than vinegar, I suppose it works more rapidly. However, ammonia can be a dangerous liquid and should be treated with respect; it is not the sort of substance to leave lying uncovered around the house if you have children or pets. If your household is composed purely of adults then the ammonia routine may well be for you—particularly if there are heavy smokers around. Adults are unlikely to lap up or stick their inquisitive fingers into bowls of ammonia.

Any liquid, in fact, has smoke-absorbing qualities. Bowls of water, strategically placed, also help keep the atmosphere reasonably smoke-free.

PAINT

A freshly painted room may be very bright and cheery to see, but it can also be a pungent one to smell for the first few hours, or perhaps the first couple of days, until the freshness has dried down.

For many of us, the pungency may be quite pleasing, or only faintly annoying. Or we may not need to use the room until the odor's full force has abated. But there are others who are seriously troubled by the smell of paint; it can cause nasal passage irritation, make people sneeze and cough, and even cause skin reactions. I know of one child who breaks out in a severe red blotchy rash if she enters a room that smells strongly of paint, and she is not unique.

Of course, opening the windows helps. But supposing it's freezing outside, or you don't want flying dust sticking to the fresh paint. Try the paint pollution remover.

PAINT POLLUTION REMOVER

1 bucket water
1 large onion

Chop the onion into chunks. Place the bucket of water in the middle of the room, and you've got it made.

It's best if you get that bucket into place before the painting starts. That way, its effect can get to work right away, rather like the vinegar-filled bowls during the party.

Dried orange peels can be burned in a metal container (such as a metal ashtray or a low-sided can) to help deodorize and clear a musty, unpleasant-smelling room. The peels should burn slowly, and I suppose lemon peel would have much the same effect since its organic components are similar to the orange's.

A swifter-burning method, better adapted to, say, freshening up a sickroom, is to put a dash of eau de cologne into a heat-proof metal dish or earthenware receptacle and light it. This works in the same manner as does brandy on a plum pudding, except that the flames keep going longer, fueled by both the alcohol and the oils present in cologne. You only need a small splash to do the trick—if you prefer measuring accurately, I would say that ¼ teaspoon of eau de cologne is more than enough. In fact, a "dash" is closer to $\frac{1}{8}$ teaspoon, so judge for yourself, depending on the size of the room. The eau de cologne should only coat a portion of the dish bottom, not fill it to any depth.

BATHROOMS

The eau de cologne method works here, of course, but quicker and easier on a day-to-day basis for removal of odors, is the burning of a match. The flames quite literally "burn off" any noxious gases, thus eliminating them.

Despite my general attitude to aerosol bombs, I readily acknowledge their usefulness in interior bathrooms or toilets in general, for example. Merely keep in mind that they possess strong ingredients and should not be sprayed too near the breathing apparatus of any living organism (man, woman, child, warm-blooded pet, fish, or even plant).

CLOSETS

We'll get to the nice-smelling things to put into closets in the next chapter, but here are a few tips for making and keeping them fresh in the first place.

Always see to it that a closet is well cleaned before you move anything into it the first time around. Then, after it's been in use, remember that a good turnout, cleanup, and sorting out not only helps keep the closet fresh but also enables you to find that odd glove and missing baseball bat.

Before replacing freshly laundered clothes in drawers or closets, let them air out thoroughly. Old-fashioned homes used to have airing closets with slatted shelves, and some of the very new ones do, too. Those of us caught in the in-between-era homes need to find our own fresh laundry airing places. It's worth locating one, for thus you can prevent unnecessary moisture from entering your drawers and closets from unaired clothes. Besides, it makes the clothes smell sweeter.

To clear out the reek of mothballs from a closet, mix alcohol and lemon juice in equal parts. Dip a sponge or cloth into the liquid, squeeze or wring it out well, and then wipe down all the interior surfaces of the closet. You could also use a vinegar and alcohol mixture.

SKUNK

To the skunk must go the dubious honor of producing what is commonly recognized as the most offensive and obnoxious odor of them all. It is unlikely that you'll find a skunk in your home, although it has been known to happen. (Deodorized, they make very gentle and appealing pets.) However, should you—or more likely, your dog—tangle with skunk spray (that incredibly strong-smelling musk that is their form of defense), tomato juice is the only answer.

And time, of course. Eventually, the smell *does* wear off. But dogs who come back from a run in the field with the unmistakable evidence of having met a skunk are best slathered with tomato juice and *then* bathed in the normal manner. Ditto any other pets or objects that get skunk-sprayed. It may take several cans of tomato juice or several squashed-up tomatoes themselves, but it's certainly worth the outlay!

12. Pomanders and Pot Pourri

If you've ever read an official bulletin on how to use pesticides, the list of *don'ts* is impressive: *don't* apply where there is danger of drift; *don't* drink, eat, or smoke until you've washed up; and *don't* spray when naked (that's not the official wording, which tends to be circumlocutory, but the implication is clear; no spraying where too much of your skin can come in contact with the stuff).

Having to go to such precautions when combating mere moths is the far side of ludicrous. It is even more so when you find out that moths have a pet hate, which is enough to frighten them away: moths cannot bear cloves.

Now, cloves are not only nonpoisonous, but also sweet-smelling and readily available. You can breathe freely around them, they will not attack your skin (should you, for example, have a penchant for moth-hunting in the nude), and they are not about to drift anywhere.

Pomanders for your closets are easy to make, attractive, and very long-lasting. They are nice as gifts, too. And the moths loathe them! What could be more perfect?

ORANGE POMANDER

You need a fresh and firm-skinned orange (the wrinkly kind tends to be past its prime), lots of cloves, and a length of ribbon.

The method is simple: you stud the orange with the cloves, packing them so close together that the orange surface no longer shows through anywhere when you've finished. Each clove looks rather like a bulb-headed nail, so that as you push the stalk into the orange, the clove "head" covers the orange skin surface around the puncture. It's a good idea to use tweezers for this job. I have done it without, and suffered from a very sore "clove-pusher's thumb" for hours afterwards.

When you finish studding your pomander, wrap it in white tissue paper and let dry in a cool, dry, and airy place for two weeks before unwrapping it. Then tie the ribbon around the pomander and make a loop with it at the top. You can hang this closet accessory from a hanger or tie it to the hanging rail itself.

It is the oil in the cloves that preserves the pomander, keeping its local environment sweet-smelling and the moths at bay.

APPLE POMANDER

Use one fresh, plump apple, lots of cloves, some ribbon—and the same procedure as for the orange pomander.

LEMON OR LIME POMANDER

Same routine—except that these small and dainty pomanders are perhaps best suited to being placed in drawers rather than suspended in closets.

All these methods are simple, decorative, and effective. If you want to get a bit fancier about it, you can roll your studded pomander in powdered cinnamon before you put on its ribbon and hang it up.

Anti-moth sachets, those spicy or sweet-filled bags of muslin that have come down to us from great-grandmother's time, are easy enough to make at home. Cloves or clove powder supply the moth double-whammy, while other spices help on the job.

Thin silk, muslin, or fine cambric are best for making all sachets. The finer ground the ingredients, the more necessary a tight-weave fabric becomes.

MOTH-CHASING SACHET MIX
Equal parts of:
cloves
nutmeg
mace
cinnamon
caraway seeds
Mix well together, then add an equal (by volume) amount of orris root (available through herbalists and some pharmacies).

Sew into small silken squares. "Equal by volume" means that if you end up with a cupful of the spice mixture, you add a cupful of orris root.

SPICE SACHETS FOR DRAWERS AND CLOSETS

You can get creative when you make your own sachet mixtures, because there are few hard and fast rules. If you choose to mix spice blends, there may be enough ingredients sitting in your kitchen right now for you to try your hand at it. Varying blends may be made with any of the following items:

cloves	caraway
marjoram	nutmeg
thyme	mace
mint	sweet basil

HERB SACHETS

Should you have a garden and your own herb patch, you can make delightful herbs-and-spice blends. The herb leaves must be dried before they are mixed into the sachet (see the chapter on herb gardens) and then you can let your sense of smell and your imagination take over.

Verbena, sweet balm, the various mints, rosemary, the savories, plus any herbs already mentioned that you may be growing instead of buying already dried from the grocery shelf, all are usable as closet and drawer sweeteners. Lavender is another long-time favorite, and here's a recipe that makes use of it.

LAVENDER SACHET
In equal amounts (by weight):
thyme
mint
cloves
caraway

Mix together and add amount of lavender that is triple (by weight) the amount of the mix.

Sachet recipes do not have to be exact, so if you prefer you can think of it like this:

A pinch or two (a teaspoon or two, if you like) each of thyme, mint, cloves, and caraway. You can also add a dash (a small dash only) of ordinary table or kitchen salt for good preservative measure. Mix together and add a cupful of lavender. No stalks, please: either just leaves or—if you have lots of flowering lavender plants—just flowers.

HERB UMBRELLAS

Lavender, savory, and mint, or any other long-stemmed herb, can be fashioned into "ribbon-weave umbrellas" that keep their fragrance longer than powdered sachets. To make these, you need the pliability of fresh stems to bend into shape, so use the herb stems immediately after cutting. You will also need a long length of ribbon for each "umbrella."

Cut the stems in equal lengths and hold them together in a

bunch, all the stem tops at the same end. Turn this end downward and tie the stems together with *one* end of the long ribbon. If using lavender, tie just below the flower position (just *above*, actually, since you are now holding the lavender upside down). If you are using one of the other tall herbs, such as summer savory, there will be leaves all the way down the stalk, so tie the ribbon at a point about a quarter of the length down from the stem's top.

Holding the herbs by the flower end, fold the long stalks down and over the short end. Now, starting at what is now the "top" of the emerging closed-umbrella shape, where the end of the ribbon is tied underneath the fold, weave the ribbon in and out of the long stems, working in a downward spiral. With lavender, stop and tie off in a bow when you have covered the flower part. With the other herbs, stop wherever the leaves begin to be big and sparse, and strip the rest of the stem clean.

Lavender umbrellas are ready for immediate use. The others are best dried by hanging in a cool, airy place before being put in cupboards or drawers. All require two weeks' drying time.

FLOWER SACHETS

If you have a flower garden or ready access to such things as really fresh roses, you can enlarge your sachet-making scope even further. A very simple flower petal sachet recipe takes only two ingredients.

Rose Petal Sachet: Heavily scented roses should be picked in the morning, *after* the dew has dried from the petals but *before* the hot sun has caused even minor wilting. Depending on where you live, this usually means some time between nine and ten o'clock in the morning of a bright day. Pick roses that are fully opened but not full-blown. Ignore buds: they'll only rot, and it is nicer to enjoy the opening of the bloom and then use it at its peak.

Once you've picked your roses, take them inside immediately and dismantle them, laying the petals on tissue paper or wire screening so that they dry quickly. This process should take place in an airy room but never in direct sunlight; drying will take several days (exact timing depends on climate, rose variety, petal moisture content, etc.). Try to prevent the drying petals from overlapping too much; bunching together slows the drying and can provoke rotting.

When the petals are dry, mix them with cloves. Whole cloves, pieces of cloves, or clove powder will do, but go easy on the amount, or the strongly fragranced cloves can overpower the scent of the rose petals.

You can tie this mixture into thin fabric bags, sew it into silken pads, or keep it in an open glass jar. As it contains cloves, it is of course one of the anti-moth mixtures.

When it comes to fragrant concoctions, the all-time classic is pot pourri. There are literally hundreds of recipes for it, some of them dating back centuries, but the basic principles are the drying and preserving of scented flowers and leaves, and the addition of yet more fragrant preservatives such as spices and oils. Salt is used as a preservative too, and many of the recipes call for it.

Like sachet blends, pot pourri can be made from many different flowers, leaves, and herbs in varying combinations. The most frequently used ingredient is rose petals. Other flowers include honeysuckle, carnations, stocks, gardenias, jasmine, orange blossoms, violets—in fact, any and all flowers that have strong and pleasing perfumes and petals that can be dried out.

Leaves (verbena, mint, lavender, etc.) are also used and both orange and lemon peel, when dried, make good additions.

POT POURRI NO. 1

For the beginner, this is a basic and simple recipe that gives the general idea of how pot pourri works.

2 parts (say, 2 cups) dried rose petals

1 part scented geranium leaves

1 part sweet basil

a few cloves (7 or 8, for 2 cups of rose petals)

1 nutmeg, grated

The petals and leaves should all be dried before they are mixed together. This mixture can also be reduced to a powdered state by crushing the leaves. Since one of the ingredients is in powdered form anyway, use silk or close-woven fabric if you wish to bag the pot pourri. Otherwise, keep it in an open, wide-necked container.

POT POURRI NO. 2

The more elaborate pot pourri recipes are usually made in two stages. The first is the mixing of the dried petals and leaves in a lightly covered container, with some salt added for perfect preservation. The second step is the blending in of oils and spices, after which time the mixture is covered tightly and left to mature before usage.

First Stage: The leaves and petals must already be dried, either by the screen or tissue paper method, or (as in the case of many herbs) by hanging in bunches. Use any selection and proportion of flowers and leaves you wish: roses, jasmine, carnations, violets, orange blossoms, lemon blossoms, stocks, lavender, verbena, rosemary, scented geraniums, honeysuckle, sweet basil, and so on.

When the ingredients are individually dry and you are ready to start the mix, get a wide-necked glass jar or earthenware pot. Avoid metal containers at all costs.

Strip all the herbs and scented leaves off their stems and stalks. The flower petals will already be separated, having been dried in this manner. Place the petals and leaves into the jar in layers one or two inches thick, covering each layer with a light sprinkling of coarse looking salt (also known as kosher salt).

When you have filled the jar (or used up all your leaves and petals) cover the receptacle well and put it away in a dry, shady place. A cupboard will do fine; just avoid direct sunlight. Let it stand for two or three weeks. It is then ready for the next step.

Second Stage: Turn out the contents of the jar into a large mixing bowl. Now, in varying amounts and combinations, add the spices and oils: cloves, orris root, mace, nutmeg, cinnamon, oil of cloves, oil of jasmine—any of the scented oils you like—allspice in powdered form, herb or perfume essences, and some gum benzoin. This is a balsamic resin with preservative properties, used both in the manufacture of perfume and in medicine.

The spices and the salt already in the mix will preserve the pot pourri adequately; nonetheless, a half-ounce of gum benzoin gives it that extra, professional and knowing touch, as do drops of essences and oils. If you can get hold of one or two of these ingredients, they are well worth using. They are now becoming easier to obtain, by mail order as well as direct from specialty stores and special departments of large stores.

Since they are stronger in their fragrance, add the Stage Two ingredients with a very light hand. As you mix, add a dash of this and a sprinkling of that. Oils and essences are to be added *by the drop*—a few drops, from two to six, depending on the amount of pot pourri being prepared, is a good guideline.

Mix gently with a *wooden* spoon, not a metal one, and replace your pot pourri in its jar. Now cover it tightly. Let it sit and mature for three to six weeks, and then it will be ready for fragrant use, either in fabric pouches or in open receptacles.

13. Preserving Cut Flowers

There are two main categories of flower preserving. First are the techniques that can be used to lengthen the life of cut flowers, thus prolonging the enjoyment of having them displayed in your home. Second are the techniques of preserving flowers and branches in dried form so that their decorative value lasts for months (sometimes even years) rather than mere days or weeks.

Both categories of preservation are ecologically sound, since both help slow down the birth-to-trash cycle. In many cases it is the speedup of this cycle within the culture of conspicuous consumption that has so multiplied our present problems. If we enjoy the beauty of cut flowers or preserved branches over a longer period of time, we are deriving more pleasure while helping to minimize the garbage problems. At the same time, the beauty of the flowers and branches thus treated adds to the quality of our everyday life. (Actually, wilted cut flowers or discarded dry leaves are not without further use, as can be seen in the chapter on fertilizers, mulches, and compost.)

And it is not valid to say that it all comes down to the same thing in the end because all flowers get thrown out eventually anyway. Anyone who cares to try the following experiment will see why.

For three weeks, buy (or cut from your garden) flowers to fill a set number of vases. (Make it just one vase if you like.) Do not help to prolong their lives; just throw them in a designated container when they're finished and let them accumulate there.

For the next three-week period, keep the same number of vases filled with flowers, but this time add all the life-prolonging ingredients and cutting measures you know to your routine. Throw the finished flowers of this period into another measuring container.

At the end of the six weeks, check to see which container has accumulated more garbage. Considering the problem of garbage in this manner, it will be obvious that a lesser accumulation of garbage is inevitable under the life-prolonging method.

A word here about plastic flowers, dyed flowers, and the tactics of some florists.

First, plastic flowers. Some people like them, and others don't, and we should all be entitled to our own opinions. They are not beauty from nature, of course, and should always be considered as coming strictly within the domain of man-made products. Whether they are considered ornaments or not, again depends on individual taste.

Gentle soap and water, and several clear rinses usually get them clean if they accumulate dust. (The very delicate fabric flowers cannot be cleaned except by a light feather duster or professional cleaning experts.)

Dyed flowers, however, are quite another matter. This is the unnatural forcing of color into a natural object and the results are most usually a sorry indictment of commercial tactics and public gullibility. A daisy steeped in blue dye is a garish parody of its original self. If one wants blue flowers, why not get blue flowers—either plastic or natural ones? Many innocent purchasers of blue-dyed daisies don't realize the flowers have been dyed—until it is too late. The streaky, wilted results are seen only at home, and then another short-lived posy lands in the garbage.

But dyed flowers are not the only tricks practiced by certain unscrupulous florists. Many of those bunches sold under a "Fresh Flowers" sign are not only getting on in life but have already been purchased and used once before—in funeral wreaths and arrangements.

There is nothing intrinsically wrong with a flower that comes from a brief stint as part of a funeral wreath. What *is* wrong is that it is for sale as brand-new, fresh bloom—and that double money is made on it. This double usage of flowers is not uncommon, by the way; it is one of those often-done but seldom-mentioned tricks of the trade.

So if you want to buy fresh flowers, try to make sure that they really *are* fresh. If they've been used before, they should be on the bargain counter.

Assuming now that you have some fresh flowers, let us turn to the methods that will help keep them fresher for longer.

GATHERING FLOWERS

If you are lucky enough to live in an area where wild flowers are still to be found, or are visiting such a region and wish to collect a bunch, take a small pair of scissors or a pocketknife to *cut* them. If you just pull at them to pick them, you may uproot the whole plant, or at least dislodge it in major degree. This usually means one less wildflower in the world.

It's best to enjoy them where they grow. Wildflowers wilt very quickly once they have been picked, some don't even last out the drive home. You could, however, collect a few seeds in the fall to plant somewhere in your own garden. There are even gardens exclusively dedicated to wildflowers, and very beautiful they are, too.

Whether you cut your own in a garden, or buy your flowers from a florist, get them into water as soon as you can. If you're doing your own cutting, it is better to take along a bucket than a basket, and have sufficient water in the bucket in which to put the stems.

If you don't have a bucket, you can use a suitably sized plastic bag. Wet it down so that drops of water are liberally scattered inside it, and place the flowers into this as you cut them. The damp, cool interior of the plastic bag will help them in that first post-cutting "shock" as well as the bucket method does.

Once you've got the flowers into the house, a prearranging soaking session in a full sink is a great life-prolonger. If you bought your flowers from the florist, rechip the bottom of the stem before placing in deep water. Not only do the flowers absorb moisture through the bottom of their stalks, but the moisture evaporating around them from the deep water helps them gain additional moisture from the air. This particularly aids any leaves and leaf sprays. Two or three hours of soaking is good: overnight is excellent. The flowers are then ready to be arranged.

When you are placing the flowers in the vase, make sure you strip off all leaves below the water line. Leaves rot quickly in water and pollute it, shortening the life of the flowers and making the water smell.

Cutting a fresh sliver, on the bias, off the bottom of the stem is also a good idea. Woody stems, such as those on chrysanthemums, should be split upwards for one or two inches, or else the bottom inch of the stem should be crushed. This speeds up the water-absorption rate and helps keep the flower fresh.

If you are using just plain water, it's a good idea to keep "topping up" the vase—that is, to add some more water to it each day. Evaporation will cause the waterline to drop and topping keeps the water supply constant.

Some flowers, however, require a daily change of water. Into this category come carnations, dahlias, zinnias, and all types of daisies. Their stalk-decay rate is swift, and changing the water on a daily basis keeps the vase sweet-smelling and the water supply adequate.

But when changing the water, do not plunge the flowers back into really cold liquid: they are used to water at room temperature, and this is what they should be given when the vase is freshened. As you check the vases, make sure that there are no stems that have gone soft and limp at the end. A little judicious snipping, and if necessary on the woody stems, more bias cutting and crushing, can keep the stem in good shape for absorbing water, and thus keep the flower blooming prettily.

There are things you can add to the water to help keep it fresh. A lump of charcoal is the simplest thing; this is often used in low, flat-bowled arrangements, where the water is minimal and where the charcoal can sometimes be disguised among the pebbles of the arrangement, or lie hidden under the blossoms that cover the surface of the bowl. It works in deep containers, too, and what it is doing is keeping down the rate of water pollution. Another thing that will do this is a dash of household bleach; a tablespoon of bleach per quart of water is a good rule of thumb. Use either charcoal or bleach, not both, and remember that it is only helping to keep the water clean, and nothing else. But if you combine sugar into the water, too, flowers tend to receive nutritive value from it.

FLOWER PRESERVATIVE NO. 1
1 tablespoon household bleach
1 tablespoon sugar
1 quart water

FLOWER PRESERVATIVE NO. 2
2 tablespoons vinegar
1 tablespoon sugar
1 quart water

Essentially, these are the ingredient structures of many of the commercial water additives. Some of them are fancier, and all of them help. For quick home use, though, the above recipes are good to have around.

When placing your flower arrangements around your home, try to keep them out of direct sunlight and drafts. The latter category includes blasts of hot air from a nearby heating outlet, or chilled waves from an air-conditioning unit. Both drafts and direct sun shorten the life and beauty of cut and arranged flowers. Apart from wilting the leaves and petals by burning or blowing off normal moisture, these hazards speed water pollution and render the flowers and stalks fragile. A bright, protected corner of the room will always display your arrangement to its best advantage while giving the flowers optimum living conditions.

Those are the general guidelines; as with most things in life, there are exceptions and specialties. Roses, for example, thrive on hearty helpings of ice cubes. After the presoak period, try arranging them in a vase filled with water and ice cubes. Change and put fresh cubes in everyday; of course they'll melt down, but that's all part of the scheme. Even in really hot weather, roses kept in daily changes of ice cubes and fresh water will keep far longer than those just plunked into a water-filled container and then ignored. Snipping off the end of the stem (again, a diagonal cut) also helps keep their water-intake process working.

Should an individual rose within an arrangement start drooping alarmingly before its time, try floating it in water. (The bathtub is the place to float really long-stemmed ones!) The problem may well be an airlock somewhere in the stalk, and a lengthwise soaking of two or three hours will eliminate this by overall water absorption by the stem's total surface. If the bloom is very delicate, you can prop it up on a sponge or a wad of newspaper.

Peonies and tulips are other special customers. When you put them in deep water for the presoak, wrap them in newspaper. You don't have to wrap each one individually; just place the blooms on a sheet of newspaper and role it up, cornucopia-fashion. Then plunge the whole thing into deep water, allowing it to soak for at least three hours.

The reason for this treatment is simple: both peonies and tulips have "heavy heads"—that is, they are heavy relative to the flowers. Therefore, it is a good idea to keep them propped up with the "brace" of the newspaper sheath while the water rises without hindrance. Otherwise, a wilted or low-water-level stalk might bend under the weight of its bloom, thus cutting off the water's upward passage.

Quite different problems assail poppies and poinsettias: they are sticky-sapped flowers, and the ends of their stalks should be sealed off *immediately* after cutting, or they will droop alarmingly and be unrevivable. The sealing off is done with heat—either by searing the stem end with a match flame or plunging it into boiling water.

Yet another individualist is the gardenia. It appears not to absorb any water at all through its woody stalk after it has been cut, but gathers what moisture it can from the atmosphere. Thus it is best to envelop it overnight in a plastic bag that has been swished through water and still carries droplets all over its interior surface. If the gardenia has been a corsage, rather than part of an arrangement, a wadding of damp cotton or tissue should also be placed inside the bag. The idea is to saturate the controlled atmosphere within the plastic enclosure, thus enabling the gardenia to absorb what moisture it can through its leaves and petals.

Another nonabsorber through its stalk is the spray of yellow pom-poms that is the blossom of the mimosa tree. Flower enthusiasts who live in regions where these abound, or who enjoy one on their own property, maintain that the choice lies between admiring the fluffy yellow bloom on the tree, or using it in the home, without water, as a drying and then a dried cut flower. So don't even bother to put mimosa blossom in a vase with water. Just arrange it in a container, and watch it deepen in color as the drying process gets to work within hours.

A flower that also bridges the gap between the arranged-in-water method and the drying processes is the hydrangea. After cutting, soak its stem in water for one hour. Then seal the stalk end by plunging it into boiling water for less than a minute (the treatment must be quick, or you'll get boiled hydrangea stalk). Then arrange it in a waterless container. The hydrangea will develop a type of iridescence as it dries and will last for months.

PRESERVING AND DRYING

We thus come to the second main category concerned with making flowers and foliage last longer in a cut state. There are two basic methods: drying (either by air or immersion in dry sand) and preserving (getting a preservative liquid to rise into the stalk). The latter method is best for foliage; the drying method can be used on both flowers and leaves.

AIR-DRYING

This sytem is much the same as that used for drying herbs. Pick the flowers and leaves you want to dry on a bright and sunny morning after the dew has dried (generally between ten and eleven o'clock). Try to pick flowers that are just about to reach their peak point of bloom. Buds tend to rot, and blooms past their prime tend to disintegrate or drop their petals before the drying process has been completed.

If the flowers are small (such as baby's breath), tie them in loose bunches by their stalks and suspend them upside down in a dry, airy, and dark, or at least well-shaded, place. If the flowers are sizable (a hydrangea, for example, which can also be dried this way, or a stem of larkspur), hanging them individually promotes better air circulation and therefore quicker, better drying.

As they dry, flowers and leaves must be kept away from direct sunlight (which will shrivel and fade them), drafts (which make them fragile and can break them), and dampness (which encourages rot). An airy closet is a good place for this process, as is the area near the water heater in a dry basement.

The actual drying will take two to three weeks. After that, arrange your flowers in a container, and enjoy them for months. A layer of sand in the container often helps to secure the stalks in the position you want.

SAND-DRYING

Although this method is slightly more complicated, it enables you to dry a much wider range of flowers. For straight air-drying, the lightweight blooms with low moisture content are best; in sand, many thicker-petaled flowers can be treated with ease, such as roses, peonies, and all the many varieties of lily.

You need fine dry sand, and a box as high as the length of your flower. Pour some sand in the bottom; suspend the flower into the box, head down and almost touching the sand, and then slowly dribble sand all around it until the box is full. Then cover the box and leave it someplace warm and dry. (By "warm," I mean average room temperature, not a cold cellar.)

Two weeks is usually an ample span of time to allow for total drying. Then comes the unpacking—and here the essential thing is for the sand to *leave* the box while moving in the same direction in which it *entered*. So what you do is open the box, hold the end of the stem firmly—and then punch holes in the *bottom* of the box, close to the edges, so as not to damage the flower head which is in the middle. Thin cardboard boxes (such as leftover cereal cartons) are best, because you can punch upward with a pencil or a ballpoint pen and soon get a colander-effect all around the bottom. The sand will run out of these holes, and then you remove the flower you have been holding by its stem end as the uncovering was taking place. Gently shake the last traces of sand from its petals, or remove them with flicks of a very soft brush (a sable paint brush will do admirably).

The bloom is now ready to be arranged in the same manner as the air-dried variety.

FOLIAGE

The tactics for drying leaves usually differ because of the size of the branches normally selected. You'd need a mammoth box and a truckload of sand for some of them! Besides, many varieties dry perfectly well if just left to their own airy devices: eucalyptus branches, for example, and lemon leaves.

Others, like ferns, do best if pressed flat between layers of newspaper. The flatter branches of dogwood, oak, beech, etc., do well if placed between thicknesses of newspaper and then put under a carpet for two or three weeks. You can capture some lovely autumn colorings this way, and have them last for much longer than their usual indoor time span.

For really long-term preservation—sometimes several years—the best method is the glycerine and water treatment. All sorts of branches respond splendidly to it—oak, magnolia, laurel, eucalyptus, and chestnut, to name only a few, and experimentation with available varieties is always interesting and frequently successful.

PRESERVING LIQUID

1 part glycerine

2 parts water

Some people prefer to heat the mixture before placing the branch ends into it, while others swear it works just as well if you use it cold. Take your choice.

Prepare your foliage by picking off any crumpled or damaged leaves. Then stand the branches in a container holding the glycerine and water mixture, making sure it reaches at least two to three inches up the stems. Within a few days you'll begin noticing the effect of the liquid as it rises in the foliage. Eventually, when it is obvious that the oil has spread all through the branch and its leaves, remove it from the mixture, wipe carefully with a soft cloth, and place it in a decorative container for display.

The coloring will have changed, the leaves will have acquired a warm sheen, and your foliage arrangement will last for ages, needing little more than an occasional dusting.

14. House Plants

There are a number of reasons why having plants inside the house is ecologically sound. For one thing, they actually help keep the air fresh and clean; during the process of photosynthesis, leaves manufacture and give off oxygen. At this time they also absorb carbon dioxide—and both steps are beneficial to the air insofar as human beings are concerned.

It is also true that in their respiration plants give off a small amount of carbon dioxide, too. However, during the hours of daylight, both the giving off of oxygen and the air-cleansing properties of the whole process more than counterbalance this effect.

House plants also help to keep the moisture balance in the atmosphere of the house. They do this partly by their living processes and partly by requiring their owner to water them if they are to survive—this also helps to put moisture into the air.

Quite obviously, house plants add a note of natural beauty to a home. They also add color and in some instances perfume as well. To be in daily contact with natural and beautiful things has a subtle influence on people; perhaps it is an unconscious stimulation of a deep awareness of life on multiple levels. We all tend to learn best when we are not aware that we are learning anything at all.

Just exactly which plants you choose to cultivate in your home depends on your tastes, the climate you live in, and how enthusiastic an indoor gardener you happen to be. Some plants are very much easier than others to grow; some require long hours of direct sunlight while others will survive very nicely in shade or artificial light. To list all available plants would be to write a complete book on indoor gardening, which is not the object here. So, apart from a few specific suggestions, the general rules of indoor gardening are what concern us.

First of all, there is the question of light. Different plants like different amounts and types of light, so be sure to check on this when you acquire your house plant or plants. For example, should you choose geraniums, or a display of cacti, you will need a very sunny spot or windowsill on which to make them feel at home. Conversely, such plants as ferns like deep and constant shade. Between these two extremes, you will find an infinite variety of plants and light requirements.

Secondly, there is the question of watering. Strangely enough, more house plants suffer from overwatering than from being neglected. If you water a plant too much, you risk it developing a conditon known as root rot. This is usually fatal—and bingo goes another house plant. I suppose it is really a question of being killed by kindness, because many people feel that—what with central heating and modern living—house plants need a good watering once a day. The truth of the matter is that they do *not*. It is far better to soak them thoroughly once a week and then let them dry out a bit for the remaining six days.

However, plants are as individual as people. Each has its own water requirements and needs, and should be treated with individual care. To test for water needs, feel the earth in the pot with your finger. If it is soggy or wet to the touch, let the plant sit without water for several days. If it is damp, don't water it that day, but keep your eye on it for possible watering within the next two or three days. If it feels bone dry, I hardly need to tell you that it needs a drink.

Perhaps the best check is the "chocolate cake" test. If the soil looks like pale, too-dry chocolate cake that you would be disappointed in if you had baked it—the plant needs watering. Another way to gauge water is to schedule it as follows: twice per week in summer, soaking well each time, and only once per two weeks in winter, soaking well each time. There are experts who say that it is very good to give plants one dormant or resting month every year, during which you hardly water the plants at all.

Many plants not only need to receive water through their roots but also must absorb moisture through their leaves. If the air in your home is very dry (and it shouldn't be, because it's not good for you either) you can humidify the atmosphere around your plants by spraying them with a fine "rain" of water; one of those window-washing spritz bottles is the ideal spray tool.

(And on the subject of spritz bottles, they are the best thing to have around a live Christmas tree, too. If you fine-spray your Christmas tree at least once, and preferably twice, a day during the holiday season, it will help it to stay green and fresh and definitely lower its potential as a fire hazard.)

Another method of keeping the air damp around your house plants is to place the pots in containers that have a layer of pebbles or gravel at the bottom. Actually, this layer serves a double purpose: when you water the plant, it allows the water to drain properly and not accumulate around the roots, and it also keeps the air around the plant moist as the water evaporates.

No plant can live in the same pot with the same earth forever. It draws nourishment from the soil and when the soil is depleted of food value, it has to be replenished. Naturally, one should not allow the soil to get into such a bad state; the process of restocking it should take place in a more or less regular manner.

One of the simplest ways is to replace a layer of the soil with fresh earth every six months. (The frequency depends on the size and variety of the individual plant.) Scoop out a layer about an inch deep and then replace this with a similar amount of fresh earth.

Or you can add compost or leaf mold. If you also have a garden, you can make these as described in the chapter on fertilizers, mulches, and compost. If you don't have a garden, your choice is more restricted, but the possibilities are still there.

For those who have neither garden nor outside space in which to manufacture their own compost, some of the following organic foods for soil and plants should be readily available within the household:

1. Cigar ash and cigarette ash, in modest quantity, are excellent additions to house plant soil. These ashes contain potassium, which is what enables leaves to remain green.

2. For plants that need an acid soil (and to know which they are, I suggest you consult your friendly neighborhood plant supplier when you acquire the plant in the first place), coffee grounds are helpful. I am talking about *used* coffee grounds: they need to be well washed—by placing them in a colander and letting water run thru them—and thoroughly dried—you can do this in a low oven. When you plant your acid-loving plant, mix in the coffee grounds with the rest of the soil.

3. Peanut shells—both the rough outer husk and the inside skin are another good household addition to the indoor garden. Mixed in with the earth as you pot a plant, they help to aerate the soil and are organically beneficial as they decompose over time.

4. Eggshells can be used in two different ways. You can crunch them up and mix them in with the soil, or you can make a liquid fertilizer from them. To make an eggshell fertilizer, you need a nonmetal container, preferably a glass jar with its own cap. Fill it halfway with crumbled eggshells and then add enough water to fill the jar completely. Cover and let it stand for three weeks in a dark cupboard and then use this liquid to water your house plant.

5. If one of your house plants is a miniature rose bush, you might keep it in mind next time you make tea. Take a leftover tea bag, add some water to it, and then give the rose a good soaking with this mixture. As a matter of fact, I have poured leftover tea on a number of different house plants and it seems to have suited all of them.

6. Beer is another natural nutrient that helps to feed house plants, so collect all those leftover dribs and drabs of stale, flat brew, add water to them, and give your plants a dousing. You can, if you like, empty the dregs from a glass straight into a pot as you clean up the place after a beerfest, but mixing the beer with

water and giving it to the plants at one of their deep-watering sessions is basically better.

Incidentally, beer should be given occasionally, and not as a regular weekly dose. All plant foodstuffs—including the commercially prepared ones you may be tempted to use—should be given at spaced intervals, and with a light touch. Natural ones, like beer, don't do as much damage if heavily applied as the chemical ones do if even slightly overdosaged. A "burning" effect can take place, which shrivels part of the plant to a bedraggled brown— which is yet another good reason for sticking to the natural rather than the artificial chemical—in all aspects of life.

Beer can also be used in diluted form as a leaf-wash and conditioner. The heavy beers are best for this; mix with water (try a half-and-half blend to start off) and wash each fully matured leaf, gently and individually. New leaves and growth do not get washed, and *never* wash fuzzy or downy leaves with beer or any other liquid preparation. Only light brushing with an extremely soft brush, or gently, low-pressure fine-spraying should ever be attempted on leaves of such surface composition.

7. Milk is a household staple that can also be used as a leaf-cleanser on solid-surface foliage.

8. If you choose to dig up your own soil someplace, rather than buy prepackaged house plant soil, you can sterilize ordinary earth by putting it in an over-proof container and baking it for one hour at 180°F.

9. If hard or chemical-loaded water is a problem in your area, there are three possible sources of excellent house plant water available to you.

(a) Rainwater. Unless you live in the middle of the desert, this supply is generally available in the necessary quantity. Collect the rainwater and give it to your plants.

(b) Snow. Depends on the region you live in and the season of the year, of course, but melted snow, when you can get it, is excellent for watering. Apart from being good water, it contains substances beneficial to plants.

(c) Your freezer compartment. You have the close equivalent of a distilled water filter operating right in the privacy of your own refrigerator! Melt down all that accumulated ice that gets removed when you defrost your equipment, and use it for your next watering session.

10. Insects and plant pests are seldom as much of a problem indoors as they can be in an outdoor garden. However, they can indeed appear. Sprays that can be adapted to use within the house are to be found in another chapter, but two house plant specifics bear mention here.

The first is alcohol, which is prime foe of the mealy bug. A cotton swab works best here: saturate it with alcohol and brush off the bugs.

The second is cigarette smoke. This works wonders in an infested bottle garden, because all you need do is blow the smoke down the bottle spout, replace the cork or cover the opening with foil, and the nicotine-laden atmosphere trapped in the bottle does the rest.

11. A crazy theory that plants grow better to music is beginning to show a basis in truth. As the theory and research stand now, high-frequency sound waves probably make plants open their pores wider and for longer stretches of time, thus stimulating their growth.

So, if there's a fiddle player in the house—try serenading your greenery!

12. As to all that "green thumb" stuff—it's much more likely to be "green breath." And all of us have it; human beings exhale carbon dioxide, and plants take this in during photosynthesis. Therefore, if you tend your plants often, and bend over them as you inspect them, you are of course breathing around them—exhaling the very substance they need. It thus seems that plants thrive for people who spend time breathing over them—precisely the people who enjoy gardening and are said to have a green thumb.

Although, as I mentioned earlier, it is impossible to list all house plants and their requirements here, a random selection of types and growing styles are included as samples of the wide variety available to us.

AFRICAN VIOLET

Despite the fact it's an old favorite, the African violet is *not* one of the easiest house plants. It has firm likes and dislikes, hates sudden change, and loathes to be moved around, rather like a fussy old lady (which may be why many little old ladies are very good at growing African violets). The following pointers are for those of us who may not yet be little old ladies but who would like to enjoy cultivating an African violet.

This plant doesn't like extremes. The temperature it thrives in can range between 60°F. and 85°F.–but no lower or higher than that.

Only mild winter sun should ever be allowed to shine on it directly. The hot blaze of summer rays can burn it to a fatal crisp.

African violets *love* humidity. This is one plant you should not allow to dry out between waterings. However, even here the dislike for extremes can be found: damp, yes; dripping, *no*. Water with lukewarm or room temperature water. This is also a plant that will be grateful for extra care in watering. Not only must you try to avoid wetting or splashing the leaves, but you should also think in terms of the best water available. Consider the rain, melted snow, and defrosted freezer supplies already mentioned, particularly if you live in a hard-water area–African violets wilt at the thought of hard water.

They do best in small, neat pots. They also like to be cleaned and groomed; a soft water-color brush will serve to flick dust off the leaves. Sitting the pots in a gravel or pebble-lined container and keeping water at the pebble level will also help maintain the gentle humidity and genteel atmosphere the plant so likes.

CACTI

There are thousands of them, in all different shapes and sizes, and many of them are marvelously easy to grow. Some are the ideal house plant for an absentee owner–that is, anyone who travels frequently and therefore has to leave plants untended for periods of time.

Many cacti like slightly acid soil, so an initial sprinkling with those washed and dried coffee grounds may not be amiss. Check first with your cactus supplier.

As to watering, too *little* water is better than too *much*. A good rule of thumb is to water in summer but hardly at all in winter. (Not a sudden change, mind you; taper off as the fall starts.) Sunshine requirements vary with the different types of cactus, so remember to check for all information when you get your plant.

GERANIUMS

Another long-time favorite, geraniums are very easy to handle as long as you have a sunshine-filled nook in which to house them. They love hours of sun and warmth.

You can let their soil dry out between waterings; they won't droop badly if you leave them alone over a weekend—or, possibly even a week.

IVY

Ivy and other leaves-only plants are highly decorative and refreshing. Ivy is also tough; it can stand a fair amount of neglect. It does like a good soaking, though, every so often, and these are leaves you can wash with water. (In fact, I once dipped a whole ivy—pot and all—into a tub of water, and it survived the incident very well indeed.)

Ivy has the additional charm of being trainable: you can make it grow around a form, such as a cone of chicken wire, to make a pleasing shape. There are a number of varieties of ivy, some are dark green and others variegated. There are both garden and indoor species of this plant; the outdoor ones will flourish inside, but I wouldn't suggest putting the indoor kind outside in anything but the mildest weather.

BULBS

To grow bulbs indoors is a seasonal affair, and they can be made to bloom cheerily when the weather and the outside landscape are at their bleakest. Normally, bulbs flower in spring, and if you have a garden you can enjoy their display from the early-appearing crocuses to the latest of late-blooming daffodils. With a modicum of technique, however, you can get many varieties to blossom indoors far earlier, some of them in December, if you start them early enough.

"Paper white" narcissus, tulips, hyacinths, crocuses, snowdrops, freesias, and daffodils are all adaptable to indoor growth. The nourishment needed for the growth of the plant and flower is contained within the bulb, so you do not need to add nutrients of any kind. What you have to supply is water and a firm base—plus a sort of booster shot before you set them in their bowls. This booster is a stint in the refrigerator. Large bulbs (narcissus, tulips, etc.) need twelve weeks of this cooling period, while small ones (hyacinths, etc.) need only four weeks.

Now, although I know I just said you do not *have* to add nutrients to make the bulbs grow, it *is* true that planting the bulb in soil rather than in pebbles and water doesn't deplete the bulb so much. So, if you *can* plant in soil, the bulb won't have to spend several years trying to recuperate from its monumental effort. I shall therefore list both methods; each produces good results.

Planting in Soil: After the cooling period, plant the bulbs in pots. The bigger bulbs must have their pointy, top ends sticking visibly out of the soil. Hyacinths, too. Other small bulbs (like freesias) are covered over. By all means plant several bulbs in the same pot if you want to, but avoid having the bulbs actually touching each other in the earth.

Keep moist and in a dark, cool place until shoots begin to show. Then bring them out into light, but try to find a cool spot for them. A window that gets sun but little heat can be ideal for some bulbs. When they flower, take them out of direct sunlight, as the sun tends to fade and wilt the flowers before their time.

If you plant narcissus and daffodils in late August or early September, then December blooms are a high possibility. The blooming time and duration varies from bulb to bulb; with good planning you can have indoor bulb-flowers from early December to early April.

After they're through flowering, they cannot be forced indoors again. People often just chuck them out, but that seems a shame.

Why not plant them somewhere out of doors? They'll either recuperate over the next year or so, putting up some leaves and eventually blooming again, or they'll decompose and become part of the earth whence they originally came.

Planting on Pebbles: For this system, you need low, flat bowls, about three inches in height. A half-inch or so of pebbles should line the bottom; you place your bulbs on this layer, being careful to see that they neither touch the edge of the bowl nor each other.

Settle the bulbs in comfortably and firmly; add water so that only the bottom section of each bulb sits in water. The top part must be high and dry. A few lumps of charcoal among the pebbles will prevent the water from polluting and smelling. As time goes by, maintain the water at its original level by adding to it whenever necessary.

A cool, dimly lit spot is a good place for an early home while the bulbs begin their growth. Then you can bring them out into the light, but keep them in a cool spot. Again, remember that the flowers will last longer if direct sunlight is not allowed to reach them.

With this pebble and water method, when the floral display is over, what you've got is a set of really knocked-out bulbs who've given their all for the flowers and leaves they produced. I still say, give 'em a chance—and plant them somewhere in the earth outside.

THE KITCHEN SINK SCHOOL OF GARDENING

I don't mean to disparage seed catalogs and "storeboughten" packets or any other form of acquiring the beginning of a plant. However, it can be more interesting to plant the seed from something you ate—like knowing two generations of the same family, and understanding their kith and kin (in this case, their pith and pit).

Some of the planting possibilities are only of educational value and short duration, so their description will be found in the chapter on children's gardening. Others, however, can develop into attractive plants of long-lasting value. Prime examples are citrus and avocado seeds.

CITRUS

Oranges, lemons, some grapefruit (not the seedless ones, obviously), tangerines, and kumquats are all workable. They are also fruits that come from trees, but you need not fear an overnight orchard crowding the living space in your house! They grow slowly, indoor conditions help keep their shapes controlled, and some, like the kumquat, are little trees anyway.

They also have attractive leaves, many of them bloom after their fourth year, and the flowers are deliciously scented. Citrus-seed plants have another strong point in their favor: they are easy to grow. Lots of sunshine and adequate watering are about all they require; no mollycoddling is needed, no special precautions have to be taken. You just plant the seeds and—given sun and water—they do the rest.

Plant several seeds of the same citrus variety per pot, since not all the seeds may germinate. Then, when the little seedlings have appeared, you can take your choice: either transplant them all to individual pots, or single out the strongest-looking one and throw out the others. Another possibility: start the seeds off in an earth-filled egg carton, one seed per section. When the seedlings appear, transfer them to regular pots. Use small pots at first; as the plant grows, you can repot it in a bigger container.

Despite their love of sunlight, citrus trees have been known to thrive under artificial light. As I said, they are hardy and eager to please—and most rewarding to the kitchen-sink gardener.

AVOCADO

These large and solid pits can be started either directly in soil, or in water first. If planted straight into the earth, the top third of the seed must protrude into the air, as it requires this split position for germination.

Frankly, I think the water-starting method is far better. You not only get a good view of what is going on, you also get to see whether anything *is* going on. If you've picked a dud seed, you'll know sooner if you give it the water treatment than if you plant it in its pot. If it isn't going to grow, the seed rots, and you can see *and* smell this quickly when it's in water.

For the water-starting method, suspend a washed avocado pit, flat end down, so that the bottom third sits in water. This is best done by inserting three or four toothpicks into the pit and balancing it on the mouth of a glass jar. Keep it in a dark cupboard, checking every few days and adding water whenever necessary to keep it at a constant level. Always use tepid or room-temperature water—*never* very cold water.

Initial patience may be needed; this stage may last for weeks, or even months. But, as long as it doesn't give off any horrible odors, just keep watching and hoping. First a root will be seen emerging from the split that has developed in the pit. Later, a shoot will begin to rise from the top, and when this shoot is about two inches high, you bring your avocado out into the light. Shaded light, mind you; no sunlight just yet.

Let it get used to its new light conditions for perhaps a week. Then take it out of the jar, remove the toothpicks, and plant it in soil. No sun allowed for another week while it recovers from the move, but *lots* of light. After that, avocados love sunshine. They are, after all, natives of tropical lands.

This plant is one that needs pruning or cutting back right from the start. What it really wants to be, you see, is a tall, single-stemmed tree, rather on the order of a flagpole with leaves. This is most likely not the shape you envision for your indoor greenery, so you'll have to be persuasive about it and use a knife or scissors. The first cut can be made when the shoot is about six inches tall: Take off the top bud only. The plant will then sit and sulk for a while, after which it will probably send up another stalk from a growth-knob lower on its stem. Whenever you trim it back after that, trim *above* a leaf or off a newly appearing crown of leaves while allowing the lower ones to remain.

Leaf mold, top layer of soil change, and similar feedings will keep your avocado going. I give mine a beer-and-water soaking every so often, and I get the impression that it'll take an axe to stop it growing now.

PART FOUR
DETOXIFYING THE MEDICINE CHEST

15. *Natural Beauty Aids*

The greatest beauty aid I know is being in love. This emotional condition imparts a glow that is unmatched by any cosmetic yet invented. But unfortunately, this desirable state is neither universally nor permanently available, and those of us who are interested in looking as attractive as we can (allowing for what Nature may or may not have done for us in the first place) have to search around for some other kind of beauty-booster from time to time.

It's best to realize right away that beauty cannot be plastered onto the skin. Certainly, a discreet touch of color or a highlight here and there can help improve the overall appearance; but beyond that, the result of cosmetics simply "layered" onto the skin is gargoylish.

Fashion fads and fancies can be fun, or silly, but they are swift to pass. There is nothing harmful in enjoying each fashion as it holds sway, but to cling grimly on to the same old styles, year after year, is just plain sad. Not to mention aging—it has been truthfully said that a woman's style of makeup reveals her true age.

What is needed for real beauty is every facet and feature in optimum condition and at its natural best. For example, nothing takes the place of really healthy, naturally shining hair. Wigs can be useful and they can be fun, but only in cases of disaster should they permanently replace natural hair. Again, hairspray may have its uses, but to spray one's hair into a state of fixed rigidity is ludicrous and, in the long run, extremely damaging to the hair itself.

Figuratively speaking, hair—like skin—takes pollution right on the chin. That is, the damaging qualities and unnatural substances in the air around us affect hair in a directly damaging manner.

Possibly the best way to approach beauty care is to think of it as being composed of two separate parts. The first is artifice, used for an immediate effect, be it paint for color or lashes for fashion. The second part, the natural, and the immeasurably more important one, is the search for deep, long-term beauty. This covers the refurbishing of the natural assets by natural means, the building up of beauty from sources within, and the cleansing and nourishing of them from without. What man has polluted, nature can restore—especially when given a little natural help. Nature also refurbishes and builds for the future; today's protection diminishes tomorrow's wrinkles, just as today's proper nutrition builds tomorrow's good health.

And health and beauty *are* linked, all the way up and down the human frame. So let's start at the top, and take a good look at hair, its care, and particularly its feeding.

HAIR CARE

Nutritionally, we can bracket hair and nails together, for the foodstuffs that are good for one are also beneficial to the other. Protein, vitamins A and B, and iodine are all essential to healthy hair and good, strong nails; translated into food terms, this means meat, eggs, lots of fish, liver, vegetables like carrots, spinach, and cabbage, cereals and yogurt, cheese and shellfish.

A salad of watercress, grated carrot, and chopped radishes is a real hair tonic. Miracles will not happen overnight. Your dietary intake should be constantly good so as to build up long-lasting strength, health, and beauty. Pineapple is another "crowning glory" food, and just about anything in the seafood line is helpful.

You can also help hair from the outside. As a start, take a long, cold look at that hundred-strokes-a-day brushing routine. It isn't *always* a good idea. Fine hair cracks and breaks beneath such constant friction; the myth that such brushing distributes hair oil evenly from the scalp is just a myth. If you have thick hair which tends to oiliness, and you find the brushing helps, go right ahead; but keep in mind that every head of hair merits individual attention, and not all scalps and hair types react the same way.

A better all-round way to achieve scalp stimulation is to massage the scalp, gently but firmly, with the fingertips. Doing this about ten minutes a day will ensure circulation and vitality under the skin, where the hair grows. You can massage it when you wake up in the morning, while you're still lying in bed. You don't need any packs or conditioners to massage, just the rubbing and movement itself.

Every so often you may wish to give your hair special treatment. The following recipes supply it with natural aids and nutrients from the outside.

Oil Massage: Work two tablespoons of olive oil into your hair and scalp. Massage all over, using your fingertips, for about fifteen minutes. Then shampoo as usual.

Protein Hair Pack: Make a paste of water and dried milk (approximately half a cup of milk powder to a quarter cup or less of water). Rub it into hair and scalp and allow to dry. Then shampoo as usual.

Brandy-Egg Treatment: This general conditioner is an old European favorite, and is applied *after* a regular shampoo and rinse. Take the yolk of one egg, add approximately three teaspoons of brandy, and beat well. After your shampoo and rinse, apply the brandy-egg mixture all over the scalp, working it through the hair and over the scalp surface with your fingertips. Allow it to remain for ten full minutes, then rinse off with tepid to warm water.

Dry hair is more fragile than normal or oily hair, and therefore usually needs more help and conditioning. The following three recipes are all dry-hair oriented, although there's nothing to stop a person with normal hair using them from time to time, and the first one can be used on oily hair, too, except that, instead of keeping the conditioner on, it gets completely rinsed off.

Dry Hair Conditioner No. 1: All you need is plain yogurt; add a couple of teaspoons (or tablespoons, if your hair is long) to your final rinse after a shampoo. Work it through your hair before draining it off.

Dry Hair Conditioner No. 2: It's another foodstuff—mayonnaise, this time. Shampoo your hair, rinse and towel-dry; and then apply about a tablespoon of mayonnaise to your scalp. Work it in thoroughly, and then leave it on for an hour. Shampoo your hair once more (using as little shampoo as possible) and then give it its final rinse, and dry.

Dry Hair Conditioner No. 3: This treatment is good for chronically dry hair as well as hair going through a temporary dry stage. Such stages can be brought about by the summer sun, by poor dietary habits over a period of time, by pregnancy, or by illness. Dry Hair, under these conditions, needs help at its growing stage, so the scalp again becomes the focal point of your efforts.

Heat a small amount of almond oil (available at the pharmacist's) by putting it in a cup and then placing the cup in a bowl or dish of hot water. Once the oil is warm, start applying it to your scalp, either by dipping your fingers directly into the oil or by using a wad of cotton. The easiest way to ensure total scalp coverage is to keep making different parts in your hair, and patting the oil along the part. When it is all worked into the entire scalp, you are ready for the second part of the treatment.

Dip a towel into hot water, wring it out, and wrap it around your head. If the towel is large enough, you can make it hold in its own heat for a while. If not, cover with a second, dry towel, to help the heat last. As it cools, remove it, redip in hot water, and apply it again. Do this two or three times over a half-hour period; then shampoo and rinse your hair as usual.

All of us have our favorite shampoos, and one of the healthiest heads of hair I ever saw was kept that way by twice-weekly washings with coco soap, followed by a vinegar rinse. (Coco soap used to be available at all drugstores. Due to changes in cosmetic fashion, this is not presently so, but I would not be surprised to see it return as we, in turn, return to our natural senses.)

The following two conditioning recipes, one of them soapless, can serve as an occasional change from regular shampoo.

Hair-Nourishing Shampoo: Beat one egg yolk and then add gradually one cup of warm water. Use this mixture instead of soap or detergent shampoo. Work well into the scalp and hair, rubbing mixture-coated hair between the hands if your hair is long. (If it's *very* long, you may need to double the original mixture.) Rinse thoroughly and then dry.

Egg Shampoo: Here you use the whole egg, plus a few drops of your usual shampoo. First, you separate the egg, putting the yolk aside. Beat the eggwhite together with one teaspoon shampoo and one teaspoon either rum or brandy. Wet your hair and rub in the eggwhite-shampoo-rum mixture. Use half this mixture the first time, rinse it out, then rub in the second half. Leave it on, and now you reach for the yolk. Rub it in carefully, working with fingertips, Allow it to remain in your hair for a full five minutes; then rinse off thoroughly with warm water. A lemon juice or vinegar rinse as a final is often a good idea.

And so we come to rinses, those final baths that remove the last traces of cleanser, that can give certain touches of their own. Softness, highlights, fragrance, and tone can all be gained from a rinse. If you live in a hard-water area, a good water softener for the final rinse is a tablespoon of borax to a gallon of water.

Shining Rinse: The addition of either vinegar or lemon juice to the final rinse gives highlights and insures the total removal of all traces of shampoo. Also, vinegar and lemon juice restore the scalp's "acid mantle"—the correct balance between acidity and alkalinity. As a rule of thumb, vinegar is good for brunettes, lemon juice is best for blondes. If your hair is particularly oily, use the citrus rinse, and increase the proportion of lemon juice to water.

Herbal Rinses: There are several of these. One method is to put a generous handful of the herb you have chosen into two cups of water. Bring to a boil, then let the mixture cool before straining.

Or, you can place the handful of herbs in a bowl and pour boiling water over them, allowing them to steep for at least fifteen minutes before straining off the herbs and using the liquid.

Camomile Rinse: Made as above, recommended for blondes.

Sage Rinse: For brunettes.

Rosemary Rinse: Fragrant, adds luster for brunettes.

Thyme Rinse: Fragrant.

All are said to be good for the scalp, and such other herbs as lavender or heliotrope can be made into rinses, too.

There are two rinses that deserve separate mention, because they combine the properties of both rinse *and* setting lotion. One is for oily hair, the other for very fine hair, and both work well.

Rinse and Set for Oily Hair: Having rinsed the shampoo out of your hair in your usual way, give your hair a last rinse, with a half cup skim milk in which you have dissolved a tablespoon of salt. Work this liquid into the hair; do not rinse out, but towel-dry and then set.

Rinse and Set for Fine Hair: A glass of beer is what does the trick. Pour it over your hair after the last rinse, towel-dry, and set. It gives fine hair extra body, and makes the work of setting easier, too. Contrary to what might be expected, this rinse does not leave you smelling like a brewery—the odor all evaporates.

EYE CARE

Even the most beautiful pair of eyes can, at times, be tired, or red, or swollen. At such times the following recipes are reliable and sound. First, one or two general tips.

By all means, wear dark glasses. Strong sun is hurtful to the eyes, and gritty cities where construction is rampant often call for glasses as protection against soot and cinders. Try not to *live* in dark glasses, however. There are days of mild light which can benefit your eyes. Be guided by comfort rather than fashion, in any matter to do with your sight.

Sometimes, a few rapid and conscious blinks can revitalize tired or scratchy-feeling eyes. Children blink more often than adults; to do so consciously lubricates the eyeball and can restore normal moisture balance. Without meaning to, we sometimes lapse into a stare (in waiting rooms, on buses, on a long and dull airplane flight) and then realize later that our eyes feel tired. That's the time to try a few extra blinks. Blinking is also good in bright sunlight if you've forgotten your dark glasses.

Eye Cleanser No. 1: A warm and lightly salted water bath is one of the best things that can happen to an eye—after all, that's what tears are. To make this solution, dissolve one teaspoon salt (preferably coarse kitchen salt) in two cups of boiling water. Allow the liquid to cool down to lukewarm before applying it to your eyes. You can use an eyecup, or a cupped hand or an eyedropper, if you are skilful at such things. Otherwise, dab the solution onto your eyes with a cotton ball or a clean, soft cloth. Blink the liquid around your eyes.

Eye Cleanser No. 2: Add three teaspoonfuls of tea to one cup of warm water. Dip a cotton ball or a clean, soft cloth, into the weak tea solution and apply to your eyes. Do this continually for two to three minutes. A favorite pick-me-up for tired eyes.

Eyelid Compresses: Swollen eyes are both uncomfortable and unattractive. They result from various sources of irritation, including crying. Tears may cleanse the eyeball, but they infiltrate and inflame the surrounding facial tissues.

Soothing compresses help here, and among the easiest to prepare are tea bags! So if you've had an emotional upset, a strong cup of tea made with two tea bags and with honey and lemon or milk and sugar will be good for your insides, while the cold, squeezed-out tea bags are just right for your eyes. Drink your tea, then lie down for fifteen minutes, a cold tea bag placed over each eye. Rinse your face when you arise; the swelling will have calmed noticeably.

Potato Compresses: A compress made of grated raw potato is another excellent remedy. This is said to help sooth baggy eyes, too—especially when the bags are the result of too much partying.

Grate a raw potato and put the pulp between two layers of gauze or fine cotton. Place the potato pads over your eyes; again, lying down for fifteen minutes to half an hour is the best way to allow the compress to do its work.

Nature meant eyelashes to be a protection, but they are thought of today more as beauty boosters. Both the health and the beauty of lashes can be improved and maintained by putting a dab of olive oil or almond oil on them from time to time.

LIPS, TEETH, AND GUMS

Almond oil is also sometimes used to keep lips smooth and free from chapping, but, in actual fact, vaseline if a far better unguent. Whether or not lipstick is used, vaseline is a good lip-coating to keep in mind. For those who do not wear lipstick, vaseline is the very best all-around lip-care balm there is.

You can whiten teeth with an occasional application of lemon juice and bicarbonate of soda. Mix these two ingredients to a stiff paste: use a teaspoonful of bicarbonate, and add fresh lemon juice, a drop at a time, until the desired consistency is reached. Apply with your regular toothbrush and brush vigorously. Rinse out with cool water.

Both the "home grown" and the "store bought" kinds of teeth respond by whitening if you use a paste of bicarbonate of soda and water. It is mixed and used just as the above-mentioned kind is.

A half teaspoon of either baking soda or salt dissolved in half a glass of water serves as a naturally cleansing mouthwash. Neither will mask heavy odors of garlic or liquor; they are merely designed to clean around the teeth and gums in a natural way.

A salt-and-water solution is, incidentally, one of the best mixtures with which to rinse your mouth after dental work, gum injury, a new tooth, or whenever a mouth antiseptic is needed. Make it a bit stronger this time—say three teaspoons salt to one cup of warm water. Use it every hour or so when the gum wound is fresh, tapering to four times a day as the wound heals.

Salt mouthwashes are excellent for the gums. This tones them up and helps keep them firm. Another aid to healthy gums is eating raw, crunchy vegetables. Gums thrive on the challenge of crisp food, and so do teeth. They are, after all, there for that purpose.

HAND CARE

Despite the foppish advice that "the best thing for hand beauty is to do nothing," stimulation through exercise and circulation is good for hands and nails and actually causes nails to grow faster. Typing and playing the piano are two examples of beneficial exercise.

It is true that these same occupations can also cause nails to break, especially if they are allowed to grow to lengths where they strike against the keys. Only individual choice and discretion can be the arbiter here—but care of nails does lead to stronger nails, no matter what the occupation.

I've already mentioned the foodstuffs that help build strong nails from within the body's system. Gelatin helps, too, but not overnight. It takes at least twelve weeks for the beneficial results of increased gelatin-intake to show up in the form of improved nail condition.

For help applied from the outside, back to two old favorites: olive oil and lemon juice. Lemon juice will help whiten nails, and it can also help in removing cuticle. Add some lemon to the softening bath in your manicure; the cleansing and bleaching effect will help get rid of excess cuticle.

Regular application of warm olive oil well rubbed in over the nail and into the cuticle will help build stronger nails and softer, smoother skin all around them at your fingertips. The next chapter gives an olive oil-salt treatment for softening the hands.

16. Skin Care

We meet the impact of the environment with the surface of our skin. It is always our skin that bears the main brunt of the climatic conditions around us. What is more, our skin also gets affected by our inner conditions. Both health factors and emotional states are reflected in the quality of our bodily covering, so the skin may truly be said to be a buffer-state between the inner self and the world.

Taking all this into consideration, it becomes apparent that our skin is something worth looking after. I don't mean one should hover over every single inch and infinitesimal lesion. But a healthy respect for healthy skin is very much to the point. If you help it weather the buffeting of climate, and see to it that its physical well-being is aided from within, you'll be doing your buffer-state the sort of service that you automatically expect in return.

Skin, like the rest of the human body, is chiefly nourished via the mouth: your food selection and intake affect its condition and quality. Also, the *quantity* you eat can affect your body covering; anyone who has been fat for quite a while and then lost a lot of weight will attest to the folds and creases of overstretched skin that just can't snap back into original shape any more.

Fruit and vegetables, yogurt, cheese, and the grains give skin the vitamins it most needs, A, B, and C. On the other hand, there are other foods that, in excess, cause trouble. Too much alcohol bloats, and too many hot spices can also cause irritation.

Many dermatologists and skin care specialists advise the drinking of at least a quart of water a day—that's four full-size glasses—and always *between meals*. This timing is essential; it allows the water greater scope in its "flushing and cleansing" action. The first glass should be drunk first thing in the morning. It's best is to have the glass waiting on the bedside table; drink it when you first wake up, and then lie back for a few minutes to do the rest of your waking for the day. The other three glasses can be drunk only a half hour before a meal but at least two hours after eating: say, midmorning, midafternoon, and two hours after the evening meal.

Deep breathing is good for your skin, and long leisurely walks in clean air help tone it up, in addition to being beneficial to the rest of the human frame. On the other hand, jangled nerves and the quick bolting of insufficiently chewed food can shortly show up in skin blemishes. Skin is a real health barometer, psychologically as well as physically.

Outside excesses to be guarded against are too much sun, bitter cold, and too much heat. Dry heat tends to be worse for skin than damp heat, but all brusque temperature changes or extremes cause skin to overwork its natural reactions, and thus exhaust its resources. Creams and oils are helpful, and aid the skin in its battle against the elements. When it comes to commercial skin lubricants, we all have our favorites; it is worth remembering, though, that the difference in price is mostly caused by the perfume that is added, and the costs of advertising.

An all-around lubricant, softener, and aid for skin is plain olive oil. (This goes for facial skin, too, as you will see in the next chapter.) It can be rubbed in, or smoothed on, or added to a warm bath. When it is washed off again, the skin will be softer, smoother, and sleeker-feeling. It will also feel more comfortable, if it had formerly been tightened by cold. Hands that are dry, rough or chapped will respond to olive oil treatment, as will rough elbows, legs, etc.

SOOTHING OLIVE OIL TREATMENT

Pour some olive oil into your cupped hand, add a few dashes of salt to it, and then rub your hands together, working the gritty, oily mixture into the skin gently as you rub. You can rub your elbows or any other rough spots of skin at the same time.

Wait five minutes. Then rinse off the mixture, using warm water and soap (preferably real soap, not detergent). You'll feel the difference right away as you dry your now-smooth and softer hands.

This treatment can be done in a much bigger, overall manner when you apply it in a skin-softening bath.

SMOOTHING OIL BATH

Before getting into the bath, rub all over your skin with handfuls of salt. This abrasive action gets rid of rough flakes, and is cleansing and disinfecting at the same time.

Then step into a pleasingly warm bath that contains a quarter of a cup of olive oil. Work the oily water into your skin by rubbing all over with gentle circular motions. You can scoop the oil into your hand, as it will always rise to the top of the bathwater, no matter how much you may try to mix it by splashing around.

When you've made sure that every inch of your skin has had its oil rub, then soap and rinse off under a shower. Again, you'll feel the difference as you pat yourself dry.

That sort of bath is marvelous for winter-buffeted skin, when the cold outside and the high heating indoors tax its oil content, elasticity, and surface texture.

Another skin-smoother is the inside of an avocado skin, which combines abrasive and oil-giving qualities. Rub it against the roughened skin surface; the oil from whatever little leftover avocado pulp may be clinging to the outer covering is excellent for your skin. Legs, arms, knees and elbows can all benefit from this method. (The avocado is really an all-purpose item, because you can eat the pulp, plant the stone, and use the rind for skin-beautifying purposes. And when you discard the rind, remember it belongs on the compost heap.)

More specifically for roughened elbows is the citrus-rind treatment. Lemon halves are best, but you can use squeezed-out orange or grapefruit halves, too. Rub them vigorously over discolored or chapped elbows; citrus fruit has both a softening and a lightening effect that smooths and clears the elbows.

You can also use orange rind to help remove discolored patches on your neck. Lemon juice, added to normal cold cream, will aid in the softening and whitening of hands, and lemon juice or a lemon half is always worth remembering when hands are stained.

After working in your garden or among your potted indoor plants, you'll find earth, grass, and plant stains come off your hands far more easily if you add a tablespoon of ordinary sugar to your soap and water. This washing trick also works on hands grimy from heavy housework.

A soap substitute that washes with gentle but thorough efficacy is oatmeal. Pour some flakes into your cupped hand, and add a little water; it will make an uneven paste, and it is this that you rub gently over your hands in hand-washing motions. Rinse off with tepid water.

Oatmeal may also be used as a drying compound. A wide-necked container of it by the hand basin will enable you to plunge your hands in after you have toweled off most of the water; rub the dry oatmeal between your palms and let it sift through your fingers. This will prevent any moisture from clinging to your skin and thus avoid possible irritation in cold weather.

But if your hands *did* get cold while still wet, and are chapped, rough, and therefore sore and smarting, try rinsing them with vinegar every time you wash them. Then dry them without rinsing off the vinegar. The smell soon fades, and the vinegar both heals and protects your skin from further winter damage.

Rubbing with the *yellow* side of lemon peel, then rinsing and drying thoroughly, also aids chapped hands.

Glycerine is also a good beauty aid to have around. On its own, a mere drop of it worked into the skin gives protective covering to hands. The hands must be dry when the glycerine drop is applied.

There's also a crazy-sounding but effective mixture that combines glycerine with kitchen ingredients:

HAND LOTION
Combine equal parts of:
ripe tomato
lemon juice
glycerine

Massage the mixture into skin by gentle "washing" motions. Do this for about five minutes, then rinse off excess with tepid water.

This hand lotion is good for normal skin. The softening protection of the glycerine combines with the cleansing, toning, and astringent qualities of the tomato and lemon juice.

FEET

If hands tend to have winter problems, feet suffer more in summertime. Cold feet are cold feet—but hot feet can be swollen, painful, blister-prone, and exhausting to the whole system. Apart from the obvious tactics of comfortable shoes, powdering, etc., here are some good foot-soothers.

Footbath No. 1: Let your feet rest under the gush of a running faucet with the water at lukewarm temperature.

Footbath No. 2: Add a cup of baking soda to a gallon of lukewarm water. Let your feet rest in this for five minutes.

Footbath No. 3: Or you can substitute salt, and let a simulated "sea water" footbath refresh you. By the way, walking through sea water, as in paddling on the beach, or walking through the surf with the water up to your knees, or wading when the water is calm—all these pleasurable occupations are excellent for your feet and are also said to be a preventative against or an assuaging factor for varicose veins.

Footbath No. 4: Two baths this time, one hot and one cold. Alternate from one to the other for about ten minutes.

Foot Rub: Peel a potato and cut it in half. Rub the potato all over your feet, using a circular, round-and-round motion as you massage. Let the potato juice dry and leave it on overnight. Next morning, rinse off with cool water. This treatment combats swelling.

CORN CURES

A really painful corn merits a visit to the chiropodist, of course. But for milder conditions, or for self-treatment until you can get to your chiropodist, the following cures are suggested.

1. Soak in hot water, then apply lemon juice nightly until corn is off.
2. Soak an onion slice in vinegar for 24 hours. Tie it to the corn and leave on overnight. Repeat for seven days. (This would mean soaking the next slice of onion on the night you applied the first slice.)
3. Tie on a lemon slice, leaving it on overnight. Repeat treatment until corn is off.
4. Tie on a slice of tomato and keep it on overnight, repeating until corn has disappeared.
5. A daily dab of castor oil has been known to help get rid of corns, as well as warts.
6. Mash a clove of garlic, apply directly to corn and cover it with gauze, securing well. Leave it on overnight. If you can bear to, repeat every night for up to fifteen nights. Curative juices in garlic work wonders on corns.

SPECIAL BATHS

There are a great many ingredients and combinations thereof which you can add to your bath water. Depending on your individual likes and dislikes, you can tailor your tub to suit your needs.

Basic functions of specific types of ingredient are:

Oils: for dry skin

Oatmeal: cleanses without soap, also softens

Herbs: for fragrance, and relaxation

Salt: cleansing and toning

Starch: given skin sleekness

Milk: you can use the liquid, or preferably, the powdered kind. It softens and smooths skin.

Cologne: for fragrance, frequently used in combination with oil or milk

All sorts of oils can be used for oil baths—olive, almond, baby oil, or any bland kitchen vegetable oil. All you need are approximately three tablespoonfuls.

Cologne can be successfully added if the oil is light and either nonfragranced or lightly so, as is, for example, baby oil. Olive oil, however, tends to have its own dominant tone; it depends on the type of olive oil, and so it is to each his own choice here. The olive-and-salt bath given earlier in this chapter is a good example: a rinsing shower and no perfume added is the accepted routine for it.

Oatmeal is best tied into a cheesecloth square or in a large cotton handkerchief. Otherwise the bath water will be full of unappealing undissolved flakes. Place the "hobo's pack" of oatmeal into the bath as you run the water. That way the soothing and cleansing qualities will mingle straight in, while the residue remains in the fabric bag.

This system is also the one to use when making an herbal bath; the twigs and leaves stay in the bag, and the oils and fragrance dissolve into the water.

Milk can be poured directly into the bath. You'll probably use anywhere from three tablespoonfuls to a cupful if it's liquid, and half a cup if it's the powdered kind. It may mix more easily if you add a little water to it first, and make a smooth and watery paste, before turning it into the bath. Cologne combines well with either kind of milk bath.

Starch, with its cool and soothing properties, is excellent in summer, and you can add cologne here, too, if you want. Salt is more invigorating in an immediate sense, although on a long-range basis it is said to have the kind of toning-up qualities that make for overall strength and therefore eventual relaxing ability.

All these bath additives are enjoyable on a year-round basis, but naturally some have extra value for many of us during the summer. This is directly due to the tanning action of the strong summer sun; some of us seek its effect, while others flee it, but in either case a bath that is soothing to the skin is comfortable for us all in hot weather.

TANNING

Tanning is a way of life to some, anathema to others. The habit has, of recent years, come under some very heavy fire from the dermatological experts themselves. A light tan, it is well known, will clear up or disguise a number of skin sins, be they blotches or pimples or sallowness from poor diet and lack of sleep. But to bake oneself mahogany brown every summer, year after year, is not so beneficial. It thickens the epidermis, causes accelerated drying, can help make facial lines into deep and permanent furrows, and slowly wreaks unchangeable havoc.

A noted skin specialist, when asked by a female patient what one should do to remain youthful, replied, "Come from a young-looking family—and stay out of the sun!" He added, "After all, how else do you make a prune?"

The gentleman has a point—but so do sun-seekers. In moderation, suntanning is good for you if you have the kind of skin that takes it well (meaning it has enough oil content of its own and is therefore easily adapted to the stronger rays). Above all, *moderation* is the key word; all those theories you've heard about ten minutes each side the first day, working up to fifteen minutes the next, and so on, are absolutely correct. And *no one* should bake for hours, even if his skin appears to be able to stand it. The damage builds up over the years—and then you get that middle-aged prune effect.

This is one of the many instances that prove the advisability of long-range planning when it comes to beauty. If beauty is skin deep, then it behooves us to keep that skin supple and fresh looking for as long as possible. Certainly it is not wise to dry it out in early youth and then go through the rest of life displaying the leathery, dessicated result.

But beauty is actually far more than skin deep, as is discussed in another chapter. As far as tanning in moderation goes, the protection of oils or tanning aids (if the sun is weak) is always a good idea. There's a vast selection of these in an equally vast price range on many a store shelf—and some equally effective substances right in your own home.

TANNING LOTIONS

We can start right in with olive oil again; its density makes it protective along with its smoothing qualities. For those who are afraid they might become akin to sardines, there's baby oil (try adding a few drops of iodine to it); peanut oil also has its advocates. When using olive or other kitchen oil, do not give in to the temptation to mix it with cologne or perfume. These can cause stains to appear on the skin, and although they are quite harmless they can be unsightly.

In the nonoily category, there's plain water, of course, and cold tea, and simple, unadulterated coke.

After a day on the beach or by the pool, one of the soothing baths mentioned earlier is also a good idea. Oil- or milk-based mixtures are ideal, as they give the tanned skin an extra smoothing.

Now what if the tan has gone too far and become a burn?

SUNBURN LOTIONS

A milk bath will help, and a starch bath will help even more—just ordinary laundry starch, the old-fashioned kind. If the sunburn is angry and stinging, mix starch and water in a cup until you have a liquid paste, and smooth this mixture onto the tender spots. You can wash it all off later, in a milk bath or in an ordinary water one—and keep it tepid to cool; don't aggravate your skin any further by immersing yourself in hot water. Let the layer of thin starch paste dry on your sunburn, and paint another layer on top if the stinging is still there.

Another home remedy for sunburn is yogurt—nice and cool, just as it comes out of the refrigerator. Spread it on the sore spots of your skin, and leave it on for awhile. When you wash it off, use cold water.

Vinegar is another first aid ingredient for sunburn. I've known it to help heat rash, too, and minor forms of sun poisoning—that red and angry irritation that is more rash than burn. Vinegar acts upon and helps balance the acid/alkali ratio of the skin surface, and is often able to calm itching and irritation.

Two more burn soothers come from your salad makings: cucumber and lettuce. Either field or Boston lettuce is best; the leaves should be "bruised"—that is, pounded lightly—and then placed on the sunburned spots. Cucumbers can be simply sliced and placed on burn spots, or peeled lengthwise and then rubbed all over the sunburned surface.

You can also make soothing lotions to apply to the sore skin.

Cucumber Sunburn Lotion No. 1: Peel a cucumber, discard the rind and mash the pulp. Mix with a little milk. Smooth the mixture over the sunburn and leave it on as long as possible or until the pain has diminished.

Cucumber Sunburn Lotion No. 2: Peel and mash a cucumber. Then measure equal parts of cucumber mash, glycerine, and rose water. Use the same way as the first lotion.

WARTS

Warts are neither painful nor necessarily unsightly, but sometimes people who have them are bothered or embarrassed by them. The following is an age-old remedy, and I have known it to work. How and why? I haven't the faintest idea.

Take a banana peel and rub its inside surface against the wart. Let the sticky substance dry on the wart. Apply again after a few hours, and again let it dry. Do this several times a day over a period of four or five days—and the wart disappears.

A daily dab of castor oil has also been known to make warts disappear.

17. *Natural Aids for Facial Skin*

Facial skin merits extra care and therefore a chapter of its own because:

1. It tends to be more delicate.
2. We are more aware of it.

We meet people "face to face"; a back blemish is often ignored while a similar mark on the face is loudly lamented. We are all most conscious of our faces as our front-line offering.

Skin is as individual in many ways as the person it covers. Its properties, likes, dislikes, and needs can be a blend of infinite proportions. Therefore, when dealing with a complexion, try to determine as much as possible by observation, both before any applications and treatments, and again after. The recipes and routines that follow are not all automatically suggested for all skins. Even when one says "dry skin" or "oily skin," one can mean a great number of varieties within these two categories.

To generalize as much as is possible: *most* skins benefit from a protective lubricant from time to time. *Many* skins benefit from "deep cleansing" methods such as facial steam baths or saunas. Some skins should only be cleansed with light oils.

And, finally, a total generalization: *all* complexions can benefit from proper nutrition. This, pointed out in the previous chapter, holds as true for the face as for the rest of the body.

DEEP CLEANSING

You do not need to have a special facial sauna in order to steam-clean your face. If you have one, enjoy it by all means; otherwise, you can get equally good results by pouring boiling water into a bowl, leaning your face into the rising steam, and covering your head and the bowl with a large bath towel. The hot moisture inside will work directly on your pores.

No matter which method of steam-cleaning you use, the addition of herb leaves to the steaming water will give that extra quality to your facial cleansing. Just how much herb you put in depends on the size of your bowl of steaming water. Experiment, and you'll soon find the amount (and perhaps the blend) that best suits you. Put the herbs in first, and pour the boiling water over them. Then move close, put up your towel, and the steam will do the rest.

Try mint leaves for toning and refreshing, camomile to cleanse and calm. Lemon peel and a few drops of lemon juice in the water will be slightly astringent; lavender will smell lovely and be gentle.

Marigold petals and nasturtium flowers are sometimes suggested for a brightening and enlivening effect. A well-known combination is a handful of mint, sage, and camomile; this is a general toner. Lime flowers, if you can get them, are another steam-facial additive. They are said to stimulate and lighten the complexion.

It must be remembered that not all facial treatments are for all people and all skins. Steaming is excellent when there is an abundant oil supply in the skin itself, but dry, thin, or exceedingly delicate skin is best kept away from such methods.

Oversteaming, even when the skin has high oil content, is not a very good idea, either. A facial sauna once a week can be right for many people, but once a day may be risking the look of a shiny boiled owl. Too much steam is worse than too little, so go easy and find the individual balance.

GENTLE CLEANSING

Some people *never* steam their faces and seldom sluice with water, doing so only to rinse off whatever cleansing agent they use.

One of these cleansing agents is milk. It is excellent for very delicate skin because it lubricates slightly as it cleanses gently and avoids all harshness. Applied with a wad of cotton, it should be patted all over the face and left on for a few minutes. Rinse off with lukewarm water.

And—here we go again—olive oil is another facial cleanser. You need apply only a very little of it, working it in with the tips of the fingers. Warm water will rinse it off; you'll need several rinses, of course.

Almond oil, lighter in weight than olive oil, is also usable in this manner. It is also an ingredient in one of the best makeup removers and skin cleansers for delicate or troubled skin:

Makeup Remover and Skin Cleanser: Pour together one part almond oil and two parts rose water. (Both these ingredients are available in pharmacies.) Shake well each time before use.

Honey Cleanser: That's the full recipe, actually—plain, ordinary honey. Or everyday extraordinary honey, if you like, because it is an amazing substance. Pure, gentle, cleansing, revitalizing, and toning, it works in all these ways both on the inside and on the outside of the body!

To use it as a facial cleanser, all you do is spread and pat it across your face, avoiding your eyes, of course. Let the honey sit there for ten to fifteen minutes; you can do another chore in the meantime, since you don't need to put on so much honey that it drips off your face—just a nice, overall film. Rinse off with warm to lukewarm water. Even the most delicate of complexions responds well to cleansing with honey, and it's good for all other types of skin, too.

Before going on to more specific masks (all of which are also cleansers in their own ways), a word about cold cream. Cold cream is the old and basic smoothing, softening, and cleansing stuff that even great grandma knew about. There are hundreds of recipes for it, thousands of variations, and a multimillion-dollar industry involved in putting out as many variations as possible. The recipe that follows is an old, and basic one. The measurements given are the kind used by apothecaries, and any pharmacist will know what you mean, should you decide to make your own. You'll need him for the ingredients, anyway.

COLD CREAM

1½ ounces spermaceti	7 fluid ounces rose water
1½ ounces white wax	8 minims rose oil
9 ounces almond oil	

Melt the spermaceti together with the wax, by placing them in a receptacle and then placing this container in a pan of water. Or you can use a double boiler if you wish. In either method, it is best to avoid letting the ingredients come into direct contact with metal. Heat-proof glass or enamel containers are suggested.

When the wax and spermaceti are melted, mixed, and still warm, add the almond oil. Then pour all this into a *warmed* mortar, if you have one, or a warmed glass or china bowl. Now add the rose water and the oil of rose. Mix well, and pour into keeping jars. These should be either glass or china or pottery or any other kind, but never metal.

FACIAL MASKS

Again, there are hundreds of recipes for these, with ingredients that range from plain mud to the exotic reaches of orchid pollen. In between, some sensible and effective ingredients turn up that, although they don't produce miracles overnight, certainly help tone, revitalize, nourish, and soften the skin of your face.

As far as miracles are concerned, mud and orchid pollen don't produce them either. It's the good, basic materials that build and maintain the good, basic beauty: egg, honey, oil, milk and milk products, and yeast. Fuller's earth, an absorbent and refined clay, is sometimes used as a carrying agent or base, but such kitchen-shelf items as oatmeal or hominy grits can serve a similar purpose. Fruit pulp is often beneficial, too. So take your pick of the following recipes and enjoy those best suited to your skin type and its needs.

Cleansing Mask for Dry Skin: Mix equal parts of baby oil and powdered milk. Rub in with gentle, circular motions of fingertips. Leave on five to ten minutes. Rinse off with warm water.

For an *alternate version,* substitute hominy grits for powdered milk. Apply and use in same manner.

Dry Skin Mask: Put yolk of egg in a bowl and beat in one tablespoon of olive oil. Smooth the mixture all over the face, and leave on for twenty minutes. Wash off with tepid water and pat dry gently.

Soothing "Mud" Pack: Mix two tablespoons of fuller's earth with one tablespoon of water and one tablespoon of witch hazel. Apply the paste liberally (avoiding the eyes: one *always* avoids the eyes, for even the mildest of masks can irritate them) and then lie down for a short rest while the pack dries. This will probably take less than half an hour. Then resoften and remove with warm water.

Pore Toner: Straight yogurt. Smooth on and leave for at least fifteen minutes. Wash off with warm or cold water (cold is more bracing if you feel like being braced) and feel the smooth difference.

Cleansing Pack: Mix a cup of oatmeal, a quarter cup of water, and two tablespoons of honey; the proportions don't have to be exact, though. Blend the three ingredients into a nice squishy paste and apply all over your face. Let the pack dry, then remove with warm water.

Whitening Mask: When your tan is fading, this recipe helps it on its way, getting you ready for the indoor look. You need an egg white, a quarter cup of plain yogurt, a teaspoonful of honey, and the juice of one small lemon.

(If your skin is dry, I'd discourage use of this recipe. Lemon juice and egg white are astringent and somewhat drying; dry skin people should stick with recipes that call for egg yolk and oils.)

Beat the egg white until it is stiff. In another bowl mix the yogurt, the honey, and the lemon juice. Then fold this mix into the beaten egg white. Apply the mixture to your face, working *upwards,* from your neck and chin, and using upward strokes. You'll see why as the masque sets: egg white has a tightening quality. Lie down and rest as the mask dries; this should take about fifteen minutes. Then wash off with warm water and finally, splash your face with cold water.

Lightening Lotion: This mixture is not as drying as the one above, and thus may be used by a broader spectrum of skin types. Take half a cucumber, peel it and mash it in a small bowl. Bring a quarter cup of milk to a boil and pour it over the mashed cucumber. Allow to cool. To apply, dip a cotton ball or gauze pad into mixture and pat the liquid all over your face and neck. Leave it on for at least half an hour before removing with cool water. This treatment should be done for several consecutive days; the milk-and-mash mix should be kept under refrigeration, and a new batch made every three days.

Fruit Packs: The kind of fruit depends on your kind of skin and what's in season. Don't bother to use hothouse exotica out of its normal maturation time; the fruit will have spent all its energy in being pushed, pulled, and forced artificially, and won't have much in the way of natural nutrients to give to your skin.

Different kinds of fruit hold different benefits as facials. To use them, you mash their pulp and apply this directly to your skin.

Oranges: restful, soothing

Lemons: astringent, drying

Strawberries: toning, brightening
Melon: refreshing, cooling
Peaches: soothing, toning
Tomatoes: cleansing, renewing
Cucumber: cooling, astringent
Bananas: softening, soothing

All such packs get left on for fifteen to thirty minutes (depending on individual reaction and liking) before being washed off with tepid water.

Neck Lightener: One must always remember that neck and face should be considered as inseparable and treated accordingly. Take a good look at both when considering your complexion; there may well be differences in skin tonality between one and the other, but they are both part of that first impression we create.

Necks sometimes get blotchy or sallow-looking. To combat this, make a mixture of one part lemon juice to two parts milk. Apply this liberally all over your neck every other night, allowing it to dry before you go to sleep, and leaving it on until the next morning.

On alternate nights use cold cream or dry skin cream or—you guessed it!—olive oil. Rub in gently but thoroughly and leave it on overnight; next night, it's lemon and milk again.

A week or two of this treatment should tone up the skin and smooth it out considerably. Sleeping without a pillow, incidentally, holds down the formation of lines on the neck.

Chin Strap or Face Lifter: The tightening qualities of egg white have already been mentioned. In an unbeaten state, egg white imparts these qualities even more noticeably. For a preparty face lift, or an overnight chin strap, merely smooth on egg white over the desired area. (Remember those upward-motion strokes.) The white will dry in less than half an hour; wash it off with cold water to help prolong the effect.

If you have dry skin, you can use the plain yolk in the same manner. It won't tighten the skin, but it will nourish and smooth it. Those with middle-of-the-road complexions can beat a whole egg and apply—thus getting the most benefit from both possible worlds.

18. First Aid

Salt, flour, vinegar, a copper penny—these are the makings of a natural medicine cabinet. That is, they are among the many average household substances that can, in case of minor ailment or emergency, help solve a first aid problem.

I am not saying that such substances should be expected to supplant the medicaments and drugs prescribed by the medical profession: obviously a doctor should *always* be consulted in cases of serious accident or illness. There are, however, numerous bodily discomforts and minor physical trials we are well able to soothe and solve on our own. A bee sting, an incipient cold, the unpleasant but nondangerous surface burn suffered by the busy housewife or the clumsy home handyman—all these can be coped with speedily and easily by using simple household remedies.

To use natural substances to cure these small ills is the best and obvious course. Also, by using natural remedies, you avoid physical pollution—for a buildup of drugs can occur in the human system, particularly if indiscriminate self-dosing becomes a habit. Unless you are medically qualified, you cannot know the full extent of possible secondary, cumulatory, or long-range effects.

A point worth taking note of is the increasing consideration given to the state of mind in connection with illness or accident. Depression, unhappiness and emotional problems can lower our resistance to infection: an often-cited theory these days is that the common cold is almost always preceded by depression. Therefore a positive and enthusiastic approach to life heightens the chances of good health. When problems come (and who among us does not have problems from time to time?) the thing is to be aware of one's possible vulnerability, taking an extra amount of physical care in order to safeguard against accident, and perhaps to prevent illness as well. As a basic illustration: if emotionally upset, be extra careful when cooking; it is far easier for the distracted housewife to burn herself.

In any event, the following natural aids and remedies are good to know, whether for self-administration or to tender to others in time of need.

ANAESTHETIC

Ice cubes are the best home anaesthetic that exists. An ice cube held to a finger housing a nasty splinter will be numb and painless in five to ten minutes. You can then go to work on removing the splinter without causing additional pain or discomfort. The ice cube method is especially handy when a child is involved. Holding the ice cube to the wound will both calm his pain and distract him.

BURNS

Burn Lotion: Add a heaping teaspoon of baking soda to a half cup of milk, and dab this lotion onto the burn with a cotton ball, clean handkerchief, or even some tissues. If none of these is available, you can use your fingers.

Burn Paste No. 1: Mix baking soda with just enough water to make the thick paste, and plaster this onto burns.

Burn Paste No. 2: Add enough vinegar to flour to make a stiff and gooey paste. Apply it to burns, plastering on thickly. Leave the paste on until it dries.

Immediate Burn Soothers: If possible, pour ice water over the burned portion of skin. Ordinary cold tap water does just fine, and some doctors maintain that city water is best because of chlorine content. Let the water continue to run over it for anywhere up to a half hour.

If cold milk is handy, use it. The average cooking burn responds well to being immersed or constantly dipped into a bowl of cold milk.

Burns and Scalds: The white of an egg, poured over a burn, holds down the inflammation and relieves the pain. The colder the eggwhite, the better.

COUGHS AND COLDS

At the first sign of a sniffle or precold heavy head, brew up the following drink two or three times a day. In some cases, it may prevent the cold from developing further, in others it will tone down its violence.

COLD GROG

1 cup water	juice of one lemon
1 whole clove	honey to taste
pinch of cinammon	

Put the water, clove, and cinammon in a pot. Bring to a boil and keep boiling for one full minute. Then turn off the heat and allow the mixture to steep for twenty minutes. Strain, reheat it, and add the juice of one lemon and a teaspoonful of honey (or two, if you like it sweet). Drink while hot.

Cold Preventative: Once again, vitamin C has been brought into the limelight. Long a favorite of health food enthusiasts, it has been described as the vitamin the body needs but cannot store. Hence the importance of constant intake.

Lately however, eminent scientists have reemphasized exactly what the health food so-called "faddists" have been saying for years: vitamin C may very well both prevent and ward off colds. Clout an incipient sniffle with all the vitamin C you can lay your hands on and if you keep the dosing up for sufficient time, you win and the cold disappears.

Tropical Cold Grog: A tot of rum, some lemon juice, and a pinch each of salt and pepper make a bedtime anti-cold grog that should knock both you and the cold out, if taken early enough!

Wine Anti-Cold Drink: Heat a glass of wine and add two cloves, a pinch of cinnamon, some lemon juice, a bit of grated lemon rind, and a teaspoon of honey. Drink while it's nice and hot.

With these recommended drinks, the main thing is to start taking them as soon as you feel the very first signs of a cold coming on. The longer you let it develop without fighting back, the less chance you have of abating its full discomfort.

This also goes for the onion trick: a diet with a high proportion of onion helps the body fight back against the invasion of a cold. There are people who make a point of serving onions frequently during the winter months, and they are positive that that is the reason they and their families keep colds to a minimum. It is again one of the examples of the season providing the food that is necessary for it: just as grapes—autumn's gift—are great strength builders in preparation for the winter that is to come, so onions, harvested late and storable for the winter, help the human frame ward off the dangers of the rigorous cold months.

If you ignored or did not notice those early warning cold symptoms, and you come down with a full-fledged bout of sniffles and such, the three essentials are:

1. Rest. 2. Keep warm. 3. Drink plenty of liquids.

Also, avoid a too-dry atmosphere. The mucous membranes of your nasal passages are having enough trouble without having to fight against dry air, too.

If you have a sore or just a "relaxed" throat along with your other cold symptoms, try gargling with warm water and salt. Another gargle mixture is vinegar and water—about a tablespoon of vinegar to half a cup water.

Coughs are often faithful companions to a winter cold; they can also appear as a solo item. Whichever their role, they are annoying and distressing. The following recipe is one of the best cough-soothers around.

Hot Lemon Toddy: Squeeze the juice of half a lemon into a glass. (Use a whole lemon if the glass is a tall one.) Add one or two tablespoons of honey. Fill the glass by adding *very* hot water, stirring as you add, and there's your toddy. Sip or drink it while it's still hot.

Exact measurements are not crucial here, so if the patient likes very sweet drinks, by all means add an extra dollop of honey (or an extra squirt of lemon juice, should the opposite be true).

Milk Toddy: Hot milk with a tablespoon or two of honey is another drink to offer the sniffling patient. For adults, a shot of whisky may be added. This makes a good bedtime drink for the cold sufferer.

DIARRHEA

Pure lemon juice, if you can take it straight, will calm things down. If you find the thought unbearable, dilute the juice with water. If you still can't bear it, add a little sugar and surely anybody can drink lemonade. The lemon juice seems to seize up one's insides and calm both the action and the griping.

Another remedy with instant calming effects is hot chocolate. However, this should be mixed with *water only*. A couple of heaping teaspoons of cocoa powder or chocolate mix per half cup of boiling water will be both strong and effective.

It strikes me as most fitting that one of the favorite French remedies for diarrhea would be a cup of hot red wine! It works, too, possibly combining the acidity of the lemon drink with the comforting heat of the chocolate one. You do not need to mix it with anything: merely heat the red wine in an enamel pan (enamel is preferable, though aluminium or other metal will do in a pinch).

Blueberries are another foodstuff that will help ease the effects of a bout of diarrhea.

HANGOVERS

Prevention is the best form of cure, and a high-calorie meal *before* a drinking party is one way to tone down the effects of the morning after. Eating *while* drinking is another way to hold down the hangover; a hearty meal or substantial snacks throughout the imbibing period will help greatly.

Another form of partial prevention is to take two aspirins and a drink of milk just before you go to bed *after* you've been drinking. It may not eliminate the next day's hangover (although it does for some people), but it should lower its force considerably.

At any rate, make it a rule that when you totter to bed with a high percentage of alcohol inside you, at least you *dilute* it before going to sleep. Drink as many glasses of water as you can get down. Alcohol causes dehydration of the body (one of the reasons you feel so horrible the morning after—that parched-mouth feeling). Therefore, the more water you get inside you, the less dehydration will take place.

But if neither temperance nor prevention was resorted to, and a hangover is a horrid reality, breakfast (or, at least, first meal of the day) can help speed recovery.

Tomato juice is a proven aid, and so is camomile tea. Soup and fruit juice as a meal is another calming combination. Liquids are good after the event, as well as before it, to help restore the balance of body fluid.

Honey helps—in fact, for some it can be the greatest help of all. It depends on the individual; what aids one slightly may help the next person enormously. In any event, all the substances mentioned here are of some help. It is up to each hungover victim to find the best individual aid, according to personal taste.

A last note: a cucumber salad, or a glass of lightly salted cucumber juice (liquefied in a blender) is recommended by many. The ingredient helping recovery in all fruits is fructose (also contained in honey).

HICCUPS

Apart from the classic method of holding one's breath and counting to fifty, there are several ways in which hiccups can be stopped. For instance, you can put a few drops of vinegar on a lump of sugar or on a tablespoon of brown sugar. Suck the vinegar-soaked sugar slowly and by the time you've finished, the hiccups should be over too.

A teaspoon of fresh lemon juice, placed in the mouth and slowly absorbed, is another anti-hiccup trick.

Drink at least ten sips of water out of an ordinary glass, but drink from the *far* side of the rim. That is, as you hold the glass, you place your mouth on the edge furthest away from you so that your lower lip is on the inside of the glass and your upper lip outside. You will find that, to be able to drink in this manner, you must bend forward. I have seen many a case of really stubborn hiccups stopped immediately by this method.

Another method you can use is to stand up straight and get your elbows to touch each other behind your back. This will probably require several jerky and spasmodic muscular movements on your part and a certain amount of effort. The combination usually cures hiccups right away.

Sucking a lemon slice is an old favorite. You can add either sugar or a few drops of bitters to the slice.

INFECTIONS

Salt is the world's oldest disinfectant. A salt-and-water solution is always a good idea for washing out minor cuts and wounds.

LARYNGITIS

Although I cannot personally vouch for the following method, never having had the opportunity to try it, it is supposedly popular, particulary in singing circles.

The cure consists of eating a whole bulb of garlic five times a day. It is said to work within 24 to 48 hours. Garlic appears in many ancient medicinal recipes, of which a large number are perfectly valid.

PAINFUL MENSTRUATION

Make yourself a hot foot bath, adding two tablespoons of mustard powder to the water. Soak your feet for five minutes, wriggling your toes as you do so. Dry them carefully and keep them warm afterwards.

Some kinds of cramps respond better to cold than to warmth. So if clutching a hot water bottle doesn't ease the discomfort at all, try a cold one. Fill the bottle with ice cubes and/or ice water, and use the same way as you do a hot one.

POISON IVY

One way of dealing with poison ivy is to crush and apply any other green leaves available—even plain grass will do. Or, you can make a thin paste or lotion of baking soda and water and keep painting over the afflicted part. Applications of very hot water to the skin areas itching from exposure to poison ivy can often relieve the local irritation. I understand that in South Carolina, ammonia is commonly used to detoxify a possible poison ivy irritation.

POISONING—UNIVERSAL ANTIDOTE

A mixture of burnt toast, strong tea, and milk of magnesia can be used as an antidote when poisoning occurs and the exact type of poison is unknown. The milk of magnesia helps battle acid poisons, while the tannic acid in tea combats alkaline varieties. The charcoal content of the burnt toast will help absorb any poisonous materials in the stomach.

The proportions to be used are, ideally, two parts burnt toast, one part strong tea, one part milk of magnesia—although these measurements are not critical. As a mnemonic, you may find it easier to recall that it is two parts of the solid substances to one each of the liquids required, and that the word "tomato" in either French or Spanish *(tomate)* gives you the clue to the ingredients: TOast and MAgnesia and TEa.

STINGS

By and large, a wasp sting is a more painful problem than a bee sting, and the trouble lies with the nature of the insect itself. A bee stings but once, frequently releasing the sting then and there, and leaving you with the sting and the poison sac. (The sad part about it—apart from the pain you personally suffer—is that the bee then goes off to die; a bee can sting and detach its sac only once, obviously in desperate fear and self-defense.)

A wasp, on the other hand, can sting many times. It will punch its stinger into your epidermis until death, fright, or a sense of caution and self-reservation make it stop. And, having jabbed its poison into you as many times as it can, the wasp may well then speed away to sting and stab another day. Potentially, they are far more dangerous than bees—unless a personal allergy in the victim complicates matters.

After removal of the sting itself, a number of substances can be applied to ease the pain and lower the inflammation. You can wash the sting in vinegar. Or make a thick paste of baking soda and water, plaster it over the sting, and cover it with a wet cloth.

Ammonia works too, so if you're at home when the sting occurs, put a few drops directly on the swelling. Another method is to cover the sting with an onion slice. This is useful to remember if you are on a picnic because you are more likely to have onions on hand than an ammonia bottle.

If you put a copper penny on a wasp sting, the pain will abate noticeably. It should all calm down completely in about fifteen minutes.

TRAVEL SICKNESS (SEASICKNESS, MOTION SICKNESS)

As far as food goes, the idea is neither to stuff nor to starve. Light, easily digestible meals are suggested, beginning a day prior to departure.

When actually en route, keep up your strength with light snacks. Avoid fats, heavy foodstuffs, chocolate, nuts, and fried foods. If traveling by car, watch the view ahead and avoid seeing the trees zip by through the side windows, as this can bring about discomfort.

Do not take in a lot of liquid before starting a journey, and in particular, avoid drinking coffee. Also try to avoid reading, especially anything in fine print.

On rough seas, apples and crackers will keep you going until the weather calms down. Avoid liquids again: these only slosh around in the stomach and make the queasiness that much more pronounced. What liquid you need will be supplied by the apples.

PART FIVE

REPLENISHING THE EARTH

19. Outdoor Attitudes

In a song popular a few decades ago, it was stressed that the natural beauties of the world belong to us all. The lyrics chose to ignore the other side of ownership—that is, the responsibility that goes with it.

If indeed it is true (and it is) that the flowers in spring belong to everyone, then it follows that everyone is responsible for them. The same goes for all wildlife, all public grounds, all areas and phases of life on this planet that belong to the community of man. And since there are so many of us, it takes awareness of this responsibility on the part of each individual before we can hope to start affecting the improvements that are presently needed.

It is safer (although not necessarily desirable) to urinate into a river than to throw a can or a plastic bag into it. Surprising as that thought may be, human (i.e., animal) waste, being organic, can be broken down and decomposed by other organisms, whether these organisms be crawling creatures or microscopic bacteria. But things like plastic and metal throw them for a loop, which is why all boating enthusiasts and riverside or beach picnickers need an extra tote bag for the trash.

All bodies of water (lakes, ponds, marshes) and waterways (rivers, streams, and oceans) should be enjoyed and respected for their intrinsic values. Use a lake as a garbage dump and it will become one—but then you won't have a usable lake any more.

Nor is it a matter of generations, or the gap between them, because a rock concert that stands for love and peace has no business filling the concert place—be it auditorium or meadow— with a thick array of torn programs, discarded hamburger wrappers and similar debris. In all fairness, it must be pointed out that unlittered concerts *have* taken place—now we need to work to make this the general rule, rather than the exception.

The day more people realize that littering is quite literally a means of throwing away their money, the litter problem will begin to decline. There are fortunes to be made in the newly burgeoning field of recycling. Cans, metal foil, paper, and plastic are all on the way to becoming marketable commodities. There are already community programs involved in this endeavor (see the chapter on the recycling of discards). The money stakes are bound to rise as recycling comes into its own.

I have no intention of getting into the great automobile engine controversy at this point, because there are plenty of experts studying and evaluating all facets of the subject. I do, however, know that there is one thing all car owners can do to help clean our air: *keep their engines clean.*

A dirty engine fouls the air far more than an engine that is clean and running in top working order. A car that is in top working order runs better and lasts longer. Therefore, to keep your car engine clean makes sense and cents.

At this stage of the game, it appears that lead-free gasoline is somewhat less harmful than lead-loaded ones when it joins the environment via the exhaust system of an automobile. As yet, I am personally unconvinced of its pristine sanctity, because lead is not the only pollutant gasoline contributes to the air, but perhaps it is a good starting point, if only to show the petro-chemical industry that consumer power is something to be reckoned with. This industry may well be the greatest of all the big polluters on an international scale.

Several million birds a year are killed because of the oil spilled into the waters around the globe. In 1969 a total of 234 oil cargo ships came to grief while afloat, spilling the killer oil liberally around the surrounding waters. Fish, seals, otters, the water organisms they feed on, and the plant life of the oceans are all being decimated by the effects of spilled oil.

The city of Venice, one of the present wonders of mankind, has recently received worldwide publicity because it seems to be sinking. There are several factors contributing to its plight, and one of them is the channel dug to accommodate the giant supertankers carrying oil to the petro-chemical center of Marghera on the Italian mainland close by the lagoon-surrounded city of Venice.

Meanwhile—thanks to the oil industry—the oil-coated beaches, the ruined waters, the fume-choked air, the belching smoke all continue to destroy or befoul the environment. Animals die, plants fade and wither, stones crumble (the "stone cancer" of buildings in Venice is caused in great part by the fumes coming across the lagoon from Marghera) all around us; each death, each destruction reflects directly onto human life on this planet, putting its future in the balance.

I readily admit that certain beetles, many reptiles, and goodness knows how many other species are not exactly handsome. Nonetheless, ugly, repulsive, or merely six-legged, all these creatures are engaged in fulfilling their work in their particular part of the chain of existence. The human race is dependent on that chain for our lives and our well-being. Therefore, unnecessary killing should be avoided.

Once upon a time (about 25 years ago) the miracle for gardens was said to have arrived. From DDT onwards, all the new, highly lethal sprays and insecticides made everything look so easy and simple. Spray it on, wipe bugs out, was the battle cry.

Today, after a quarter of a century of solid spraying, gardens are no more bug-free than they were before. And we've also developed some brand-new problems—thanks to precisely the sprays and insecticides that were supposed to solve everything.

Obviously, something wasn't taken into consideration.

That something, too long neglected, has now come into focus. It is the delicate balance and intrarelationship among all the living organisms and species of this world. They all exist to some purpose. They are food, shelter, or a combination of both to other species while they, in their turn, get their nourishment and protection from yet other species. To "wipe out" a species is to destroy a link in the chain of nature. This is not only senseless and foolhardy—it is downright dangerous. Dangerous to *man*, I hasten to emphasize: a threat to human existence in this world.

Therefore, when dealing with your personal corner of the earth—be it a garden, or a planted terrace, or a row of plant pots on a window sill—consider everything in terms of reasonable balance. No one wants a backyard positively *crawling* with bugs, but the truth of the matter is that a sprinkling of some of them is not only a natural phenomenon, but also a natural necessity. Our gardens *need* bugs, not in hordes, but in proportionate numbers. Bugs are bird food; bugs pollinate flowers; bugs' bodies decompose and become part of the earth again. Some bugs, along with being so useful, are beautiful besides. (You don't believe me? Well, how about butterflies?)

Bugs *out* of proportion, however, are another matter. A cascade of caterpillars can munch your cabbages down to stumps in no time, while an army of ants marching through your garden can be as destructive as any other army similarly occupied. Therefore, I am not telling you to sit back in hopeless resignation and watch the hordes go by while your garden becomes a disaster area. What I *am* suggesting is that you use ruses and recipes that are both effective *and* safe. By safe, I mean safe to nature at large, and to all the other species around. If you want to get rid of a bug on a leaf, by all means do so, but *without* destroying the leaf, the plant, several songbirds, and the neighbor's cat besides.

RUSES

First of all, you can hold down the insect population of your garden by employing a few simple ruses.

FRIENDS

As a start, always keep in mind: "Toads and birds are a gardener's best friends." These creatures can destroy an amazing amount of insects, spiders, and grubs. When you consider that a bird eats about a quarter of his own weight in food *per day,* you'll realize that even the smallest sparrow is a pretty hearty eater.

To encourage birds in your garden, remember to feed them in winter if you live in a cold, snowy climate (see next chapter also). Then the birds will have the habit of dropping in for an snack, and they'll polish off your unwelcome garden tenants in a trice.

In addition to being essential to us in the all-inclusive chain of existence, birds enrich our lives by adding beauty in the form of color and song. Let us enjoy them on the wing: no dust-collecting birds' eggs display locked in a sterile showcase can ever compete with the real thing out in the open where it belongs. To watch a bird's nest in all its stages, from the time the parents-to-be build it right through the hatching and feeding of the fledglings until they finally learn to fly and go their own way in life—such sights are unforgettable.

Toads—gentle creatures despite their odd, pop-eyed appearance—do a great job of gobbling up all sorts of crawling things down at ground level. They're a good staple in any garden, and usually like making a small, damp, and secluded corner their base, from which they hop forth to eat when the mood strikes them. They are unassuming and gentlemanly in their habits, and one is seldom even aware of their presence.

Lizards, if you live in an area that has them, are also a boon to the gardener in controlling bugs.

Down at the level of bug-eat-bug are two species which have recently been put on the market. These helpful insects are ladybugs and praying mantises. Nursery gardens either have them or know where they may be ordered. The ladybugs lay eggs toward the end of their own life cycle, and so the next generation of spotted garden-helpers comes free.

PLANTS

There are certain plants that will ward off a wide variety of insects. If you plant these around or among tender plants that are usually targets for hungry bugs, you'll help protect them.

Curiously enough, several of the "protector" plants have strong-smelling leaves or flowers, or general growth. Herbs planted as protectors will help keep the marauders down. Garlic, chives, and onions are guard plants; so are sage and savory. Thyme borders can also help.

Pyrethrum planted around roses or anything else will keep many insects away, including ants. Ants can be among the most difficult of insects to cope with; just a few in the garden—

especially around your compost heap—are quite beneficial, but more than that amount can create a problem.

Marigolds are bug-repellers, too, along with being cheerful and colorful. Their strong, almost earthy smell is akin to that of many chrysanthemums, some of which (the less exotic varieties) are also guard plants.

TRAPS

Sow bugs, sometimes called woodlice, are those little gray armadillo-like things that roll up into a ball for protection. If your resident toad hasn't eaten in their corner of the garden lately, or the woodlice are creating a nuisance among your potted plants, you can make a potato trap to collect them.

Potato Traps: Take a fair-sized potato and cut it in half. Scoop out enough of the potato so that, when you turn it flat side down, you have an "igloo." Also scoop out a little "door" in the side of the spud, leading to the hollow inside.

Place your potato igloo in woodlice country, and they'll walk right in through that igloo door. Soon you'll have a potato full of woodlice—and at that point I suggest you throw the whole thing into the compost pile.

Other Insect Repellents: Light can either attract or repel insects, depending on the insect—and on the light. A bright white bulb will bring many a wing fluttering around in no time at all; a yellow bulb will have few fans around it.

You can use light to great advantage if you enjoy your garden during the cool summer evenings, or like eating out on the terrace. Match the bulb to your needs: yellow near the table will illuminate the food, while discouraging most pests; a white or blue bulb some distance away will keep the bugs busy and out of your hair.

Oil of citronella, long recognized as a mosquito repellent, is sometimes blended into the wax of a heavy candle which can then serve both to illuminate and to guard.

If you live in a land where the chinaberry grows, you have a natural fly-repellent at hand. Branches of this tree (technically, the Melia Azedarach) always hang over an outdoor summer fruit stand

I know of, and nary a fly dares to crawl over the fresh-picked merchandise.

Beer Traps: You may find it hard to believe—but slugs love beer! All you need are flat receptacles, like old soup plates or jar covers, and some beer. Fill the containers with beer and place them on the ground in the slug-infested area in the evening. Next morning, they'll be full of slugs. You can dump all that into the compost heap, too, but better give it a turn with the pitchfork or rake, to incorporate the new additions properly.

RECIPES

As this is being written, there is already at least one good organic bug spray on the market and several others in the final stages of premarketing tests. So if you must buy your garden aids, look for the organic ones to do the job.

However, there are a great many mixes that can be made at home easily and simply. They are effective, specific, and, above all, ecologically sound. That is, they do their specific job and no more; by using these recipes, you will not be filling the earth with poisons that do not break down for ages, lurking there to kill off harmless species.

The following recipes are a selection of on-target remedies for garden maladies, time-proven, safe, and sound.

ANTS

Ants can be a hindrance inside the house as well as in the garden. They are always difficult to get rid of, and even the most lethal poisons do not eliminate them forever. You can control your ant population just as well by nontoxic methods.

Method 1: You'll need equal amounts of borax and confectioner's sugar for this. Mix them well, and sprinkle wherever there are ants. If you know where their nest-entrance hole is, scatter the mixture liberally around there. This method is best used on nonsoil surfaces and in places that do not get rained on—that is, indoors, or in sheltered places, or on brick or stone paths.

Method 2: If you locate the anthole, pour boiling water down it. (This method is *not* suggested for use indoors!)

Method 3: If you locate the anthole and can dig down to get at the nest itself, do so and then make a wet and sloppy mudpuddle out of the spot by pouring a mixture of kerosene and water, in equal parts, over the dug-up area.

APHIDS

Soap and water, frothed and sprayed on roses is excellent against aphids. It is nontoxic for other insects, but the aphids cannot breathe through the film of suds. Following are some other sprays you can make yourself.

Onion Spray Chop onions finely, or put them through the blender. Measure the resulting mash and add an equal amount of water. Spray this mixture on both outdoor and indoor roses that have become aphid-infested. The onion smell fades, and so do the aphids.

RHUBARB SPRAY
3 pounds rhubarb leaves
3 quarts water
1 ounce powdered soap
1 quart water

A word of caution here: please remember that *rhubarb leaves are poisonous for people,* too. Handle them with respect and keep them out of the reach of children and pets.

Chop the leaves, put in a pan with three quarts of water and boil for a half hour. Strain off the liquid through an old nylon stocking and set aside to cool. Mix one quart of cold water with the soap powder, then add to the cooled rhubarb-leaf liquid.

This mixture is used full-strength as a spray against aphids. The same recipe, slightly modified, combats clubroot. Simply omit the second, soap-and-water addition. Pour the rhubarb-leaf water over the soil before sowing plants that can be afflicted by this disease.

Tomato Spray: Crush tomato leaves and either boil as above or soak in water for 24 hours. Use directly as a spray.

BORERS

Ash Paste: Save the ashes from a wood-burning fireplace, mix with enough water to make a thin paste, and apply generous coating of this to the affected trees.

Copper Nails: A word of caution: this method, although it is effective against borers, must *never* be used on fruit- or nut-bearing trees, which absorb the copper traces into their flowers and then into the edible growth. People who eat fruits or nuts that are loaded with copper become very ill indeed, so go back to the ash method if borers are ravaging your orchard.

But if you have a hawthorn, for instance, that has a nasty case of borers, hammer in a handful or two of copper nails all around its trunk at its base, flush with the bark. The rising sap will dissolve the copper and carry it through the plant's system, killing off the borers as it goes.

SLUGS AND SNAILS

I've already mentioned the simple beer trap method, but here's a boosted mix for this operation. You'll probably collect moths in this one as well, often those who lay the eggs that turn into voracious caterpillars.

Any wide, shallow, and slippery container will do for this method, just as with the one described earlier. Sink it level with the ground, and fill with the following mixture:

1 part water

1 part beer

molasses or brown sugar

If you use a cup of each liquid, a tablespoon of either molasses or brown sugar would be in proportion. And there's no need to open up a fresh keg of beer; slugs are not fussy, and the collected leftovers from someone's beer glass will do fine.

The resulting moth-and-slug mess you find the next morning can also be added to your steaming compost heap.

As far as snails are concerned (and slugs, too), you can go in for wholesale slaughter with no greater weapon than a handful of salt. Salt dissolves them, and a sorry sight it is, too, to the soft-hearted gardener. However, the salty remnants of a snail or slug will neither poison wildlife nor pollute the soil, so this method works within the scheme of things if you have to combat these creatures.

SPIDERS

Spiders are among your good friends in the garden, so there's really no need to wipe them out. There are, however, some people who have a horror of spiders. If you are among those, powdered sulfur discourages spiders and prevents their presence. It does not actually kill them, merely encourages them to take off in a tremendous hurry.

For big fat hairy tropical spiders, I would suggest the business end of a shovel or the nearest long weapon that is handy.

EARTHWORMS

Must you kill earthworms? They are good for the soil under normal conditions, and the commercial worm-killers are both dangerous and of long-lasting effect. Experienced gardeners all maintain that worms are among the gardener's best friends. But if for some reason you feel you have to get rid of some of the worms in your garden, for heaven's sake, don't use preparations that contain chlordane. It not only kills the worms that you are trying to eliminate, but it also continues to kill off more worms plus other species and organisms for *the next fifteen years.* In effect, preparations such as this one turn your garden into a veritable poison-pit.

Soil that has had chlordane poured onto it cannot be used for vegetable crops such as carrots or asparagus, or any other edible root plants for at least two years. Even government bulletins hold dire warnings about chlordane around food plants; if all you are after is a couple of earthworms, to use chlordane is akin to killing a fly with a cannonball. Worms that are only partially poisoned by this muck may be eaten later by a bird, then pass the poison into the bird kindgom. Chlordane accumulates in their bodies and the eggs laid by these birds are infertile. It is in this manner that a species can become extinct, and we have already lost too many kinds of birds forever.

There is a lesser danger to human beings, but it is a danger nonetheless. Chlordane can be absorbed through the skin. The effects of its being deposited in the body are not as yet threatening, but even a passing sickness is unnecessary and unpleasant.

If you have to get rid of some of your earthworms, do it this way:

Mix one ounce of potassium permanganate in one gallon of water. Pour this mixture over one square yard of ground. The worms will come up to the surface, and you can then just sweep them up and dump them on your compost heap or, if you insist on getting rid of them completely, throw them in the trash can.

Turning from specific cures to more general, all-purpose sprays, let us begin with one of the easiest to make right in your kitchen. Apart from being easy, it is also a preparation that has wide-range effect.

PEPPER-ONION-GARLIC SPRAY

4 hot peppers

4 large onions (or six small ones)

2 bulbs of garlic

Chop, grind, or mash these ingredients together and cover with water. Let the mixture stand for at least 24 hours and then strain off the liquid. Add enough water to this liquid to make a gallon, and there you have your all-purpose spray. It works on a number of plagues and pests that attack vegetables and flowers including roses and such temperamental plants as azaleas.

The above spray—lethal as it may be to bugs—is perfectly harmless to human life. This next mixture is not: nicotine, no matter how you slice it, is a toxic substance. Therefore, when making this spray, be sure to wash your hands before touching food and keep the finished tincture in a bottle marked "poison."

ALL PURPOSE NICOTINE PESTICIDE

4 ounces regular cigarettes OR ½ pound filter-tipped cigarettes

1 gallon of water

Put these two ingredients in a pot and keep at a rolling boil for a half hour. Remove from the fire, and allow the liquid to cool down. Then strain it through a nylon stocking and store in a well-covered bottle.

This is the tincture which is diluted with water to make the pesticide spray. A good proportion to use is one part nicotine tincture to four parts of water.

Keep in mind that this spray is a toughie; if you use it on vegetables, do so at least two weeks before you plan on eating them, and wash them thoroughly before doing so, of course. Conversely, when you have one of the larger, more difficult pests to get rid of, the nicotine spray is just what you need. Caterpillars are among the species that succumb to its influence. Hibernating greenfly can also be eliminated with this preparation.

Along with its versatile applicability, this spray also has the advantage of being extraordinarily cheap for the smoker, since the tincture can just as well be made out of cigarette butts as whole cigarettes: so you see, the contents of an ashtray are all recyclable, since ashes are good for soil, butts are good for making pesticide, and all the contents put together can also be thrown onto the compost heap for reintegration into the earth. The one exception would be any filter tips in the ashtray; they are fit only for the garbage can.

RUSSIAN TEA

This mixture is excellent against black spot on roses and potato blight. It is made by soaking one part of dry animal manure in ten parts of water. Let the mixture stand at least 2 hours before using, and strain before spraying on the plants.

We can all be our brother's keeper in this respect, swapping knowledge as we acquire it and trading tips on how to conserve and beautify the land. The first step in this direction would appear to be a heightened awareness of nature, which is something that is enhanced by pure observation.

One last point about observing: should you be a beach or rock enthusiast, remember to replace any large stone slabs you may displace to observe the goings-on underneath. All sorts of creatures live, nest, lay eggs, and reproduce under the shelter of a rock.

20. *Birds, Bees, and Butterflies*

Anyone who has a garden can exert influence over the ecology of the neighborhood far beyond the borders of his own domain. Even those who are city dwellers with a terrace, a balcony, or a well-set window can often add to the health of the cycle and the strength of links within the connecting chain of all that is live and natural.

That birds are both receivers and forwarding agents of this ecological influence has been of growing interest for many years. Birdbaths and feeders adorn many a garden and the birds congregate around and embellish the places that welcome them.

What is less known is that you can also attract butterflies to your garden, and surely there are few more beautiful sights to see among the flowers. Different climatic regions house different varieties of both birds and butterflies, yet some of these varieties travel very far indeed. Many migrate; some reproduce in one area and winter in another. Wherever they are born, or live, or fly to, however, birds and butterflies need nourishment.

That goes for bees, too—and they also are essential in the natural chain of life. Their defense mechanism may make them somewhat less popular than the birds and butterflies, yet they play a necessary role in life on this planet. So if you have a garden, you'll welcome them into it and be glad to see them helping the pollination as they help themselves to nectar, the basic ingredient (along with pollen) of their honey industry in the hive. One of their favorite blooms is the blue one that appears on borage, the herb used in summer drinks, in salads as a condiment, and in the preparation of pickles. Borage grows well in sunny, dry places, and will resow itself from year to year.

Bees also love things like honeysuckle and clover. Clover, incidentally, is a weed, and in passing, I'd like to say a word or two in defense of weeds.

Weeds also have their place in the scheme of things. They are food for the birds and insects, homes for insects and essential bacteria, and at the end of their vegetable cycle decompose and break down to enrich the soil from which they took their own nourishment. It is true that they do not have to be straggling all over our cultivated gardens, but to try and wipe out weeds entirely is a foolhardy attitude.

If the garden is big enough (and only personal opinion can determine this), a patch of wild and unkempt growth in a corner somewhere need do no harm and may do much good. At the far side of the compost heap, the ground may favor a tangled, self-seeding growth of weedy intruders. And I know of a city balcony, surrounded by thickly polluted air, where a lushly green pot of healthily leafed plants makes an attractive sight. These plants are doing their bit toward refreshing the air by helping make oxygen—and every last one of them is a purebred weed!

Sometimes our gardens have weed patches that we didn't plan, and if yours has a clump of stinging nettles in its midst, you just may have a butterfly breeding ground going there. Many butterfly varieties lay their eggs on these plants, so that when the caterpillars are born they can start munching on their favorite food. Other weeds favored (mostly for nectar food) by butterflies include goldenrod, clover, all sorts of wild daisies, and dandelions. Thistles are also great favorites; again, it is a question of climatic region and variety of butterfly that will determine which butterflies and which plants you may have.

Nonetheless, the plants that most interest the garden enthusiast who likes butterflies are those that are recognized garden varieties. They will encourage butterflies to stop by and feed, but not breed.

First of all, it seems that butterflies, along with liking flowers with high and suitable nectar content, also have color preferences. Yellow and purple are their main passions. This proves out in their weed favorites: thistles are mauve, clover is mauve to purple, goldenrod and dandelions are yellow. A butterfly may well ignore a huge white rose (they don't much care for roses, anyway) and rush to the nearest purple lilac bush. They adore lilacs, preferring the purple to the white, of course, but settling for and on the latter if the former is not available.

Marigolds are also great favorites (these cheerful, orange and yellow flowered plants are all-around benefits in any garden); and in the shrub category, the buddleia bush is also known as the butterfly bush because of its great popularity with these pretty creatures. Wallflowers, alyssum, sweet william, and sweet rocket are butterfly-attracters, as are the beautifully scented phlox flowers, and candytuft and mignonette.

As can be seen from this selection, butterflies prefer the simpler blooms, some strongly perfumed, to the man-perfected hybrids that have been bred away from the normal development within nature. This tends to make a butterfly-attracting garden a far easier place to tend and grow than a rigidly specialist and exacting selection of so-called "show" flowers. They can be fun, too, if horticulture is your passion—but if what you want is a garden you can relax in and enjoy without spending too much time and energy, why not plant it accordingly.

For example: do you really want a lawn? If you do—fine. Go ahead and plant or sow or sod one, water it and tend it and mow it. And mow it. And mow it.

If you don't want to get involved in this kind of work, why not consider other forms of ground cover? They do exist, from random stone paving interspersed with low-growing plants (often used as border plants) to pachysandra. I know of a charming garden where one whole corner, under a very large plane tree, is paved with widely spaced hardwood tree trunk slices. Between them, wild strawberry plants blossom and fruit profusely, while one section to one side of this unusual spot is carpeted with violets.

Imaginative? Yes—and also easy to maintain. For every climate and for every yard or garden or terrace, there are ways of planting it and setting it out so that its owners reap the maximum benefit from it, according to their chosen mode of life.

Back to butterflies: there are a number of herbs that they love, too, which you may want to include in your garden. Lavender and verbena are two favorites. Heliotrope in the warmer regions attracts the butterflies of the area, while rosemary, valerian, and catmint are more general flourishers. Catmint, by the way, is also a bee favorite.

Should you have fruit trees, and should some of the ripe fruit open and drop to the ground, the butterflies are almost sure to come crowding to the feast. Since they live only on sweet liquids, the juice of such fruit is a banquet indeed. Should the fruit have begun to ferment slightly, the butterflies will be in seventh heaven! Curiously enough, such indulgence does *not* seem to make them drunk.

Keeping in mind the functions you want your garden to fulfill, how about planting a tree or, if it's big enough, several trees? They help supply our oxygen, and they use up much of the carbon dioxide belched out by factories and breathed out by people.

Trees are also living filters; they trap and tone down dust, pollen, and numerous other irritants. They also regulate the humidity in the air around them via their respiration processes, and they lower its temperature, too. All of us have known the relief of cool shade on a blazing summer day; again, the tree is a physical shield from the hot sun itself. Trees also form shields against wind and sound. The list of their virtues goes on and on. Trees affort protection in many different ways and, in equally varied manner, they also afford protection to birds. A garden with a tree or two in it is far more likely to attract birds than one that is a flat expanse of low planting. Most birds get nervous in wide-open spaces when they are close to the ground; they prefer protection.

Some trees offer more than others, to birds' as well as to home owners. Climate and region and some bird species are all factors to be taken into consideration. Some popular trees for birds are birches and conifers, native cherry trees and dogwood, the hawthorns, flowering crab, spruce, hemlock, and mountain ash.

When selecting a tree to plant on your property, be sure you know as much as possible about the tree you are considering. Trees, like people, come in all types, shapes, and sizes, and they have varying habits that need to be taken into account. Try to choose a tree that suits your surroundings and purpose. A long talk with a nurseryman should help clarify all the essential points.

Shrubs, too, offer protection and often food to the birds, while offering beauty to the people who enjoy the garden. The viburnums are one such category, numerous berry-producing shrubs are others. The hollies—and there are not only several kinds of these, but male and female varieties as well—are bird-attracters.

Pyracantha (perhaps more popularly known as firethorn) is another favorite; bayberry, coralberry, snowberry and the multi-flora rose also go on the list.

Since soil and climate determine what will grow best with least trouble, it is well worth asking the experts before you do your planting if you are a novice in gardening. Not only are there garden clubs that provide information, but there are also nature-oriented societies that give out excellent information for free, or for a minimal sum.

Whether or not you have room for trees and shrubs, don't overlook the advantages of some of the vines. They can disguise an ugly wall, grow where there is little room for more demanding plants, and decorate vertically—and all while beckoning to butterflies and birds. Virginia creeper, honeysuckle, trumpet vine, and grape are widely different in type and bird-and-butterfly appeal, all successful in their natural growing regions.

And with the mention of honeysuckle, we're back to the weed patch again, for some of its varieties grow like weeds and spread like them, too. But there are other weeds, mentioned earlier in connection with butterflies, that also appeal to the bird popula-tion. So, if you can, leave one unkempt spot to its own devices, and it will also do its bit toward populating your garden with welcome visitors.

Despite their differences in seed and dietary requirements (remember, birds will be your best friend in the anti-bug department), there is one common need that all birds share, and that is water. If you can provide it for them, they will inevitably gather. This is easy enough in warm or temperate weather; there are many attractive birdbaths, and even a pie dish sunk into the ground or affixed on top of a pole, or a similar container suspended from a tree can be effective.

Freezing weather, however, presents the ice problem. If the birdbath is near the house, and you have both the time and the desire to do so, the pouring of warm water into the bath, or boiling water over the ice layer that has formed, will keep the birds going. This is probably the best method.

Another method is to rig up a special winter bath unit with a night light candle under it. You can make a protective square with bricks, fashion a candle-shield out of an empty can (cut out top and bottom, punch some holes in the remaining surface for air circulation) and place a long-burning candle inside the can and a bird bath on top of the whole structure. The brick "walls" hold up the bath and protect the candle holder; the idea, by the way, is to keep the water from freezing, *not* to overheat it. A change of candles and the regular addition of water is all the maintenance needed.

Do *not* add substances to the birdbath water itself to keep it from freezing. You risk killing off the very creatures you are trying to help.

If you also want to put up bird feeders during the cold months, remember that, once started, such welcome aid to birds should be continued for the length of the winter season. Birds, like all animals, are creatures of habit, and once accustomed to finding food in a certain spot, will return to it with clockwork regularity. Should this food source suddenly cease to exist, there can well be loss of bird life before the group can locate other sources of nourishment, if it is even possible for them to find other food in the bleakness of winter.

Simple feeders and birdhouses are described later, plans for more complex structures are readily available from bird societies and publications. Not all birds are attracted to the same winter-supplement foodstuffs, of course, but you'll find a large selection will eagerly feed when you make available such items as mixed seed (sunflower, millet, cracked corn, etc.), suet, and—of all things—peanut butter! Leftover cooking fats mixed with seeds make popular meals for some birds, and some of them will not scorn a leftover doughnut.

Should you put up birdhouses—that is, secluded and protected structures suitable for nesting—you will be able to enjoy watching the care and rearing of the next generation. Many species of bird make really dedicated parents and watching them get their fledglings to fly is an unforgettable experience.

One note of warning: birdbaths, feeders, and houses should never be located in such a position that the birds are placed in danger from a marauding cat or dog. Cats are natural hunters, so are most dogs. So do not tempt birds into your garden solely for them to become prey for your house pets. Birdbaths, feeders, and houses should all be situated well above ground so that they are inaccessible to the climbingest cat.

A last note: when spring cleaning time comes along, and you wash your wool blankets rather than having them dry-cleaned, hanging them outside to dry or air serves a double purpose. First, the air-freshening qualities of sun-warmed wind cannot be beaten, and second, the fluff that wisps off the blankets will be picked up by birds and used as lining for their nests. No doubt wool garments similarly aired will benefit the birds in the same fashion. It's nothing but a scrap of discarded fluff to us—but no doubt it's heaven to a baby bird.

21. Fertilizers, Mulches, and Compost

If you have a garden, you are in a unique position to improve the ecological balance of your surroundings. In so doing, you will clear the air, enrich the soil and the balance of nature—and have the loveliest, most enjoyable garden around.

No two ways about it: plants that are grown organically are, in the long run, the best of all. This is easiest to see in vegetables—or, rather, to taste, because those that are organically grown *do* taste better than the ones that are chemically forced. On a long-term basis (and little is done overnight in a garden, as all enthusiasts know) flowers, shrubs, and trees will all show the advantages to be reaped from use of natural fertilizing methods.

No matter what size your garden, there are always positive steps to take in the right ecological direction. Natural fertilizers, mulches, and compost are the mainstays of the natural garden. The first two are applicable to the smallest garden, and I have heard of penthouse gardeners who made compost in a corner of their city terrace. With a bit of ingenuity, a compost heap can be managed even in the smallest garden.

NATURAL FERTILIZERS

These are often referred to as organic fertilizers, for they are all organic material, being recycled into the earth. The many manures come into this category—horse, cow, poultry, sheep, etc.—as do all the mixtures that are made of natural components.

A historical example of organic fertilizing is the story of the American Indian who taught the early settlers in New England to plant some fish along with their corn. The Pilgrims followed his advice and harvested good crops as a result—and fish meal is used to this day with satisfactory results. As a matter of fact, the recent urgency of pollution control has given birth to a profitable new business: the conversion of seafood waste (the discards of seafood canning and packing plants) into agricultural fertilizer.

Organic fertilizer does more than merely nourish plant growth. It also restocks the soil—that is, as it decomposes, it *becomes* soil in conjunction with the other components present. Therefore, the earth derives full enrichment from it, instead of a partial and temporary boost.

The earth that grows the best plants is made up of the following mixture:

45% inorganic components (sand, ground rock, i.e., minerals)
50% air and water (yes, earth does contain air)
5% organic matter, also called humus

It is this last 5 percent that you can enrich in your own garden. Chances are you started off with soil that had a lower humus percentage; with a little care and adequate organic fertilizer, you can grow well-nourished garden plants and keep the organic matter content of your soil up to par.

Leftover beer (already discussed in connection with house plants) and tea (both the liquid and the used leaves) are natural aids for the organic gardener. The beer gets added to a watering-canful of water; give the drink to whichever plant you feel needs a boost. If all your plants are doing fine, distribute it indiscriminately.

Tea is more specific; roses love it. If you use tea bags, rip them open, and either collect the used tea leaves in a container until you have enough to place around the bottom of your rose bush or plants, or deposit the contents of each tea bag as you use it. Teapot users can just add water to the teapot after it has been used and swill out all the remaining liquid around the leaves at the base of their roses.

LIQUID FERTILIZER

If you have a lawn, there's a very simple liquid fertilizer you can make from the mowings. After you've cut the lawn, rake or sweep all the cut grass together and put the pile into a bucket. Fill the bucket with water to the height of the grass. Set this mixture aside and let it ferment for a few weeks. You will then have an excellent liquid fertilizer which can be used on all your plants.

LEAF MOLD

Leaf mold, another top-grade nutrient, is even easier to make and it does more than add richness to the soil. If you can make leaf mold, you are actively preventing one of the worst forms of air pollution—the smoke that rises from autumn leaf bonfires.

To burn leaves is madness of major proportions: it is to destroy valuable additives to the soil itself, denying nature's part of the very cycle that keeps life going. And it is also to pour pollution into the surrounding air. Bonfire smoke has been described as containing far more cancer-producing elements than the smoke from cigarettes.

So set aside a small section for a leaf pen, and reap the eventual benefits by letting nature take its own course.

Take the dry and discarded leaves that exist in small measure throughout the year and become abundant during the fall when deciduous trees and plants shed their foliage. To convert these leaves into leaf mold, keep them in a small pen where they will decay and change from dry leaves into rich fertilizer.

If there's a shady hidden spot where nothing much will grow in your garden, you might like to use it for your leaf pen. All you need are three or four posts and some wire screening. Its height, shape, and size depend on your ambitions and the space available. Naturally, it also depends on how many leaves you can expect from whatever area you are sweeping or raking.

The wire (chicken wire is usually adequate) is only there to prevent the leaves from blowing away. There is no constructed bottom to the leaf pen; you can dig down a few inches and make a trough for the leaves if you like, but it's not necessary. You rake up your leaves, dump them into the enclosure—and then you just wait. Time and nature will do the rest.

Add only fallen and dry leaves No branches, no pulled-up weeds—those go on the compost heap, about which more later on. Crunch down your pile of leaves by stamping on them. Collect them in the fall; if the next summer is hot and dry, water the decaying leaf pile every so often.

Wait through a second autumn and winter, and then your leaf mold is ready for use. Some leaves will decay more quickly than others, so you might get a pile that is usable after only nine months or a year of rotting. The mold is very good for house plants too, as it is rich in content yet fine in texture.

MULCHES

A mulch is a layer of something put *on top of* soil—either between rows of plants or around their individual bases. Its purpose is multifold: mulching prevents a hard layer from forming on the soil, it can discourage certain pests, it slows down the rate of evaporation thus keeping moisture well in the soil, and, if the mulch used is organic, it eventually decomposes and enriches the soil by becoming part of it.

Nonorganic mulches are sometimes used, too (gravel around single shrubs, etc.), but it seems a pity to forego the far greater benefits gleaned from using an organic one. Hay, lawn clippings, peanut shells (or other small nutshells), straw, leaves (same process as the making of leaf mold), and pine needles are all possible mulches. I have also heard of seaweed being used for this purpose, either dried or well washed before being utilized; its high nutritive value makes it top quality humus when it eventually breaks down and joins the soil. Grain discards such as rice husks are also mulch material, so if you live in an area where grain is processed, you might look into the possibility of getting these cheaply.

The regulatory effect of mulching is extremely beneficial;

summer sun scorches the mulch instead of dessicating the soil beneath. Also, many mulches slow down the development of weeds. (But don't sneer too unkindly at these unwanted intruders, for they are marvelous additions to your compost heap. Even weeds have their value in the overall scheme of things.)

The time to lay out the mulch is once the seedlings of the annual plants are up high enough so you can see them (a couple of inches should be ample). Then apply your mulch layer; established perennials will probably need a new layer, too.

Give everything a *good* watering—a sprinkling of water every night is just about worse than useless. Give plants a good soaking, and then leave them alone for a few days. This is especially important where lawns are concerned; a good four-hour soaking once a week is far, far better than twice-a-week sessions of two hours each, for example. The main reason is root development. If the lawn gets a thorough soaking, the water sinks far down into the soil and the grass roots grow deep. They form a strong and solid root system, able to draw moisture and nourishment from the lower levels.

With light sprinkling or short-time watering, on the other hand, there isn't enough water to soak down very far. Further, much of it may evaporate. Only the shallow layers of soil get to absorb any moisture, so the roots develop at a shallow level. where they are too easily harmed by any problems that come along. Shallow roots simply do not have the strength and stamina of deep root developments and the lawn itself will show the difference as time goes by.

COMPOST AND COMPOST HEAPS

Despite the school of organic gardening thought that says mulching is all you need, there's a hard-core community of compost users. The addition of compost does make marvelous soil with excellent humus content, the sort of soil that grows the sweetest-smelling flowers and the tastiest of vegetables.

The building of a compost heap has the added advantage of recycling many different materials that are commonly regarded as garbage. Garbage, like beauty, is often in the eye of the beholder.

Kitchen wastes like carrot tops, squeezed-out orange and grape-fruit halves, moldy and inedible refrigerator-incubated leftovers, eggshells, potato parings, apple cores, and any of the food discards of the average household are manna for the enthusiastic builder of a garden compost heap. The compost heap can be said to epitomize the whole ecological process: waste is put to use by being recycled into the total scheme. A carrot top, whose lower root has helped feed people, is reprocessed via the compost heap so that it may turn into humus and, in turn, nourish a newly planted crop of carrots through its new role as an integral part of the earth.

All of which is interesting and heartening in theory—but how does a compost heap *work?* And how does one make a compost pile?

HOW COMPOST WORKS

Quite simply, compost is an accumulation of organic debris that, with nature, time, and an occasional assist in the form of added specific ingredients, breaks down and decomposes until it is a black, crumbly, nutrient-rich additive that joins the humus content of any earth you add it to, thus enriching the soil in a total and enduring fashion.

A compost heap quite literally "cooks down." Its heat is generated organically from within and as the pile heats and rots, its bulk becomes less.

The whole process sounds smelly, you think? But it isn't. This is not a pile of stinking garbage smelling because the sun is causing the gases of surface decomposition to fill the surrounding air. This is purely organic matter decomposing *from within,* by breakdown and heat. It is the very heat that prevents dangerous bacteria from forming. The organisms that do exist within the steaming pile are all working toward the formation of the finished compost product.

HOW TO MAKE COMPOST

You don't need a very big space to make a compost heap. Just a bare patch of earth, two feet by two feet, can provide an adequate base for a compost pile. Even if you have the space, I would caution against building too huge a compost heap. Compost heaps should be neither too small nor too large, for two reasons: 1. manageability; 2. obtaining the right temperature. It is far better to have several small heaps than one big one, though your decision must depend on what space you have available.

For the actual building, there are several methods.

Pit Method Stake out your space and then dig it to a depth of at least two feet. Remove all the loose earth. Build your compost heap within the pit, watering between layers and major additions. Cover with heavy sacking or plastic sheet and hold down with bricks.

The idea of covering a compost heap has several purposes. It keeps moisture in, helps develop the necessary heat, prevents winds from blowing the pile around, and discourages flies.

Flat Method Just clear the required space of surface and build your compost pile upon it. After additions, you can keep everything in place by covering it with sacking or plastic as mentioned above.

Note: It isn't necessary to cover a compost heap, and many gardeners, especially those working with fairly large compost heaps in large gardens, do not bother. However, covering the pile makes it "work" faster and therefore turn into good usable compost much quicker. In large gardens there are usually several compost heaps, each at a different stage of development, thereby ensuring a steady supply of this organic fertilizer.

Box Method This is the enclosed system; you can build a wooden compost box, or use an old oil drum or a plastic garbage can (if yours is a small garden). The enclosure can be topless or covered, but it does need air reaching it from below. Prop the box or whatever up on two rows of bricks and drill holes at the bottom of the container. The draft that comes in from the bottom is essential to the heat-producing organic and bacterial breakdown.

If you build your own compost box, just build sides and set it up on slats or special bricks and get your built-in draft that way without bothering to make a proper box-bottom.

So much for space and enclosures. Now for the contents.

Compost Making: Compost is not a delicate concoction; how much you put in of any of the acceptable ingredients is not crucial.

One of the basic activating ingredients is manure; from one-quarter to one-third of the pile should be composed of it. What kind? It doesn't matter particularly, so long as it is *fresh.* Chicken or pigeon droppings are excellent, but very strong. Never put fresh droppings of this type near plants; however, it is excellent when mixed into the compost heap, for its very freshness helps activate the organisms in the pile. If the manure is not fresh, then you may need a commercially packaged activator, although semi-dried manure plus watering can sometimes work just fine.

When you water the compost pile, your aim should be to keep the heap damp and heating, but not so soggy and dripping that it "drowns" and cools down. How often you water it depends on the climate you live in and how much matter you add to the heap—also, whether or not you cover it; obviously, an uncovered pile will need more frequent watering than a covered one.

Starting the compost pile with a layer of small twigs and branches is a good idea, as that helps the air get up into the pile. Next, some inches of small greenstuff—lawn clippings, pulled-up weeds, picked-off leaves, vegetable waste (those carrot tops again), and so forth.

After that, a layer of manure to get the working started—horse, steer, poultry, rabbit, dog, pigeon, etc.

Next, maybe a sprinkling of earth. (If you dug a pit for your pile, you can keep some of that earth handy for this purpose.) Although not essential, thin earth layers are a good idea after you've added manure if your compost heap is anywhere near your neighbor's property line. It will help cancel any organic smells and lessen the chances of complaint.

And then you're off and running. Remembering to add manure every once in a while, just pile on all the organic garden and kitchen refuse. Your pile will grow as you add to it, and sink down as the matter decomposes and the compost forms. Within a month, you should see this black, rich, and crumbly nutrient forming in the pile. Depending on the time of year a compost pile is built, it takes from four to six months to have it turn into workable fertilizer. An old broomstick kept stuck into the compost heap will feel good and warm to the touch when the temperature of the compost heap is correct.

Acceptable garden matter includes all lawn and grass clippings, leaves, weeds, rejected vegetables or fruit (but smash thick things like cabbage stalks first). The finer the matter, the quicker it will break down.

Dry leaves make bulk, but it's the green vegetable matter that helps keep the pile working. If you have a leaf mold pen going, too, I'd suggest you put dry leaves into that and reserve only the greener ones for the compost heap. Or put *all* leaves into leaf mold and then all your other vegetable matter will take care of the compost.

The home ecologist's dream material is the leftovers from kitchen and table that can be recycled right back into the earth. The thing to do is to have two garbage cans in the kitchen, one for the stuff that will go on the compost heap, the other for the trash that is either incinerated or carted away. You'd be surprised how easy it is to get into the two-garbage-can habit. I know of families where even the under-fives know which throwaway goes where. The rim of a peanut butter sandwich goes in "the garden can"; the paper wrapper from a lollipop goes in "the trash."

A plastic garbage can with a removable inner pail is best for your garden-bound goodies, as you do not line it with paper or plastic, but simply tip out the contents directly onto the compost heap. Then wash out the bucket, and start fresh.

What goes in the bucket? All vegetable and fruit parings, peelings, tops, and leaves, tea leaves and coffee grounds (you can toss in tea bags as well, because that paper will decompose), eggshells, nutshells, and all fish leftovers including fish bones.

But not leftover meat, which has too much grease. And no meat bones! The following incident will illustrate the reason.

A flourishing compost heap in a large New Jersey garden had been the recipient of all kitchen leftovers, including a rather heavy lamb chop bone. The garden, bordering as it did on the neighboring woods, was often the romping ground of the local wildlife, and the owners of the garden often enjoyed watching everything from birds to field mice to moles and woodchucks. No one knows exactly which breed discovered the large lamb chop bone. However, something did, and it must have made good gnawing.

Unfortunately, the sated gnawer discarded his chewed-out bone in the middle of the driveway one evening, where it was later discovered by the homeowners when it pierced the front tire of an automobile, causing a thunderous blowout. No one was hurt and no damage was done, other than to the left front tire. The bone had pierced through it like a gigantic thumbtack.

If you do want to utilize the very real nutrients in bones and meat, get a pickle jar or gallon jug and put your leftovers inside with enough water to cover them. Then seal the jar and store it away in the attic or basement for a few months. Bacteria that are always in the air will decompose the meat and a good part of the bones into a fairly clear, nutritious (to plants, naturally!) soup that you can pour off as needed. This method works well with any dead fish from your home aquarium. Put them in a jarful of water, and within a few months they will almost completely disappear, leaving no offensive odor behind.

You can also empty your vacuum cleaner bag into your compost-bound pail, and, if you cut your family's hair, all hair clippings go in, too. Ditto the hair or fur brushed out of human heads, or pets' coats.

A friend who is a long-time garden enthusiast once wrote to me, in answer to my query about compost: "All vegetable refuse, newspaper bits, carpet sweeper dust, grass cuttings—babies' disposable diapers *(superb!)* Cindy's [a Samoyed] messes, plant clippings, horse and poultry manure *(superlative!)* and if you happen to have a privy ... *(divine!)* ... *Faute de mieux,* a occasional light dressing of sulphate of potash to activate and ... patience."

Which is pretty all-inclusive, to say nothing of casual. And it works like a dream, as my friend's garden proves.

There are, of course, some things that should *never* be added to the compost heap. Cans, metal bottle tops—in fact, metal of any kind—man-made fibers (nylon stockings, brushes, rags), too much newspaper (my friend said "newspaper bits" meaning occasional shreds thereof), broken china or glassware, and of course, *no plastic.*

In addition to watering the compost heap, there is also the question of turning it. If you do, you can keep a better check on how it's getting along, spreading the "working" sections nicely throughout the heap and thereby getting it all going, but you may have to water it a bit more. If you just let it sit there and stew by itself, you won't have to exert yourself to turn it with a rake or pitchfork. On the other hand, it isn't back-breaking labor exactly, and to see the workings of each different stage is always interesting.

CITY-BRED COMPOST

Suppose that, instead of a garden, you have a small terrace with potted plants, or a smaller balcony and some window boxes. Can compost and leaf mold be managed here? The answer is, certainly it can: it is merely a question of adaptation.

Leaf mold is the easiest; a wooden box, tucked in a corner surrounded by pot plants, makes an ideal cache of crunched-down dry leaves. Just leave them alone until you repot a plant; then a handful or two along with the soil will help matters greatly.

Your leaf supply is abundant too, if you just stop to think about it. I'm not talking about the stray samples that float onto your terrace; I'm referring to the huge piles that collect in parks and tree-lined streets. No one will mind a dedicated gardener loading a basket or a bag with leaves. If you're shy, do it in a group, or pick up the leaves one by one as though you were a botanist collecting specimens. Or get kids to help you; kids are less self-conscious about things like that.

Mulching is possible for pot plants, too. It depends on what they are and where they are placed as to whether it is advisable or not. And decorative cover (pebbles, gravel) might be more desirable in any event, helping to retain moisture in the earth but not adding to its humus in any way.

As to compost: if you have a large terrace and a secluded,

little-used corner—why not? Get a plastic garbage can (but not the kind with a removable inner section) and make some air holes in the bottom. Then place layers of screening and some balled-up chicken wire inside the container; you need to get air up into your compost, remember? After that, you build your layers much as you do in a garden heap, keeping the pile damp and always replacing the cover. Keep a box of earth close, so you can sprinkle some over any pungent additions, and also see to it that the heap gets its ration of activating manure.

A last note for the garden plot compost maker: earthworms are good for compost. They're also pretty good for the garden in general, because, among other things, they aerate the soil. So don't stamp them out—and if you haven't got any in your part of the soil, why not look into getting some from an earthworm nursery? They do their share in the cycle of nature and living—just as we all do when we garden with compost.

22. Herb Gardens

Herbs need soil, sun, water, and a modicum of care—and very little else. In return, they will give you flavoring for your food and scents for your sachets and closets. While they grow they are decorative and frequently both colorful and perfumed; once harvested, their useful life is long lasting indeed.

You can grow them in a sunny corner of a garden or on a windowsill that receives light and sunshine for several hours a day. There are some herbs that can flourish on a lot less than that; I have had healthy pots of parsley and chives do very well on less than one hour's direct sunshine per day.

Depending on where you live and what your method of growing is, different selections of herbs can be easily cultivated and enjoyed. Certainly all of us can grow a few of the kitchen basics near windows indoors; outside herb gardens vary in type according to the climatic conditions.

In recent years there has been a tremendous upsurge of interest in both the growing of herbs and their uses. Herbal teas have again become increasingly popular of late.

ANISE

This is an annual, with many uses. Tea can be made from its fresh leaves, and its seeds are found in such things as bread. Anise is also used in candy, and on the commercial level a liqueur is distilled from it.

BASIL

Basil is also an annual and it needs lots of sunshine. You can use it in both fresh and dried form; it has long been famous as a teammate for tomatoes. Basil-flavored vinegar is easily made by pouring hot wine vinegar into a bottle containing several sprigs of fresh basil. Let this infusion rest for three weeks before using it.

BORAGE

Also an annual, but quite hardy. The showy blue flowers are sometimes candied, like violets, but the more conventional uses include the addition of a few tender borage leaves to lemonade and similar cool summer drinks.

CARAWAY

By herb garden standards, this is one of the taller plants, for it grows to about two feet. It is biennial, its harvest taking place in the second year. The seeds are used in both sweet and salty foods; breads and cakes can be flavored or decorated with caraway and it is also an ingredient in certain cabbage dishes and stews.

CHIVES

Chives are members of the onion family and are usually more delicately flavored than their bulbous cousins. The plant is perennial and it grows to a height of approximately six inches. Chives blend with and enhance meat and poultry dishes, many vegetables, and all green salads.

DILL

A tall annual, this is a distant relation to celery, although its flavor is more distinct. Both the leaves and the seeds may be used in cooking; the former blend with fish and salads and add flavor to the humble boiled potato, and the latter are used in making pickles.

MARJORAM

Marjoram and oregano are cousins, and there are several varieties within the family. These tasty herbs, some of which are annual, are most often used in dried form and are basic flavorings for meat and poultry dishes, eggs, vegetables such as peas and beans, and occasionally for green and mixed salads, too.

MINT

There are several different kinds of mint, all of them perennial, most of them hardy. Some crave more water than others and I have known of flourishing mint patches growing like weeds in a damp corner near a leaky garden faucet. Mint's multiple uses include sachet-making, summer drinks, mint jelly, and tea-brewing.

PARSLEY

One of the kitchen basics, parsley grows easily and quickly in pots as well as in the garden. Ornamental parsley has curlier leaves but somewhat less taste than the flat-leafed variety, but both have innumerable uses. All savory dishes and such things as poultry stuffing benefit from the addition of chopped parsley.

ROSEMARY

This is a perennial and a strongly flavored one at that. It is also strongly scented and therefore is usable in sachets and pot pourris. When cooking a dish with rosemary, care must be taken to add it sparingly. It can be used with lamb, poultry, and game. It is also sometimes added to dried bean dishes.

SAGE

This is another strongly flavored perennial and its use is most commonly associated with poultry and poultry stuffing. However, it can also be brewed as tea, and teams well with cheese, sausages, and vegetable dishes.

SUMMER SAVORY

An annual, savory should be added sparingly to meat and vegetable dishes. It is used in salads and salad dressings and certain egg dishes can also benefit from it.

TARRAGON

This plant is a sun-lover and grows well from cuttings, which should be planted in well-drained soil. Tarragon vinegar is made by the usual infusion method: pour hot wine vinegar into a container housing tarragon leaves or, better still, one or two full tarragon stems, leaves and all, and allow the mixture to rest for three weeks before using it. This enables the tarragon flavor to permeate the vinegar. Tender fresh tarragon leaves are a special accent in green or mixed salads and dried tarragon can be put to this same use. Both fresh or dried leaves may be added to mayonnaise.

THYME

This is another of the famous kitchen basics. It is a perennial with a wide range of uses. All meat and savory dishes can have thyme added to them, and its dried leaves are among the staples used in pot pourri.

The above herbs are all culinary additives although some of them are also used cosmetically (rosemary can make a hair rinse) and for perfuming purposes (in pot pourri and sachets). There are other plants that can be included in a herb garden with uses that are exclusively connected to their fragance.

Lavender is one of the old-time favorites and there are a number of sweet-smelling geraniums whose perfume lies mainly in their leaves. Heliotrope is not hardy and may need a little extra care, but it repays it more than amply by the special quality of its fragrance. Lemon balm is also strongly scented; it prefers to grow in partial shade and can do very nicely in poor or sandy soil.

Marigolds are frequently found in herb gardens, too. Apart from their bug-repelling virtues, marigolds give cooks a colorful additive for salads or stew: a *light* sprinkling of marigold petals provides golden-orange accents and subtle flavor.

There is a variety of camomile that can be used as a ground cover, whereas another type grows tall. Each has its uses; individual selection depending on your herb garden's location is suggested here. Camomile tea has long been used as a sedative for stomach or nervous disorders.

An old-time favorite in making of cough-calming candy is horehound. It also makes tea that is soothing to the cold-sufferer. To use horehound, pick the leaves just before it blooms, so that the foliage is at its peak of flavor. For tea-making, pour boiling water over the leaves and let this infusion steep for five minutes before drinking. You may flavor the tea with lemon or honey. Two cups of water per ounce of leaves is a good infusion proportion. You can make the infusion stronger by adding more leaves when you prepare it for mixing up a batch of cough drops.

HOREHOUND COUGH DROPS
1 cup horehound infusion
1½ cups brown sugar

Mix well and bring to a boil. Then let the mixture simmer and boil down until a test drop of this liquid put in cold water forms a hard ball. Butter or oil a baking dish and pour in the mixture. As it cools, mark it into squares with a knife, dipping the knife into cold water and then drying it as you work. Alternately, you can oil the knife lightly; the point is to keep the hardening candy from sticking to the metal.

Break the square into individual pieces, dust with confectioner's sugar, and keep in an air-tight box, preferably lined with wax paper.

Like marigolds, nasturtiums are not plants we immediately associate with herbs, and yet their place among the herbs is quite justified. Nasturtiums grow easily and love the sun; in return they give you pungent leaves to add to salads and you can use the developing seeds, after the flowers have gone, as part of your pickle-making mixture. The red, gold, and yellow blossoms of the nasturtium may also be used to decorate dishes, including salads.

To the herb specialist, the above selection and suggestions may seem like child's play. To the middle-of-the-roader, enthusiastic but at times uncertain, I hope it may serve as a general guide. To the nervous beginner, to whom all herbs are a mystery but who would like to try anyway, I would suggest a pot or two, grown either on a sunny kitchen windowsill or in an easily accessible spot on the balcony, terrace, or garden. Once you see how easy and enjoyable it is, you'll feel far more sanguine about embarking on a garden planting, or a full array of pots, or even a multi-herb planting in a large container indoors. A compact garden format is the wagon wheel herb garden: you simply put a wagon wheel flat on the ground and plant different types of herbs in each space between the spokes.

A tasty and earthless planting that can appeal to everyone, from the most experienced of gardeners to the rank beginner, is an indoor crop of mustard or cress, usually referred to as mustard-and-cress, and usually grown together. Actually, these two plants belong, basically, to the same family, the *Brassica* bunch. (Watercress is another cousin.)

You need two seed packets: one of curled cress, and one of white mustard. You also need a flat dish, like a baking dish, and a growing surface—paper towels or napkins, a wad of cotton, or some layers of flannel will do fine. Put your growing surface flat into the bottom of the dish. Wet it till it is evenly and thoroughly damp, but *not* watery. Then sow your seeds on top of that. If you are planting both kinds, and want to use them together, plant the cress first. Then wait four days. The cress will already have sprouted by the time you plant the mustard.

All you need to do is keep the growing surface moist. When the little plants are three to four inches high, cut the crop, rinse under cold water, and add to your green salad. Mustard and cress are pungently flavored and add a distinct accent to a mixture of lettuce and other salad ingredients. Mustard and cress go well in sandwiches, and are both attractive and tasty when used to garnish hot or cold main dishes. Furthermore, raising a crop of mustard and cress is enjoyable and encouraging. There's only a two-week span between sowing time and your indoor harvest—and it just goes to show how easily one can learn to develop a green thumb.

PART SIX

SAFEGUARDING THE FUTURE

23. Babies

Tradition, religion, and superstition notwithstanding, the need for a stable world population grows more evident by the day. It is not only a question of upholding living standards; we have now reached a point where the survival of the human race will be at stake in the not too distant future.

We cannot crowd the earth and its finite resources with ever-multiplying billions of mouths to feed. The facts of the matter are as simple as that. Statistics are available to prove what will happen if we don't slow the birthrate to a reasonable pace. And please note the phrase is *will happen,* not may. As more and more people are becoming convinced of the need for a lower global birthrate, more and more interest is developing in methods of selecting the sex of a child. It is presumed that this will eventually become a scientific reality. Right now, sex selection of babies is still at the research stage. But there are a couple of methods already known about that raise the chances of getting one's choice of boy or girl, although naturally these methods do not guarantee 100 percent accuracy.

Interestingly enough, when nature is left to its own devices, about 105 boys are born for every 100 girls. Of course, the 105/100 ratio is on a worldwide basis; it varies from one region to another, and is not therefore applicable everywhere. Furthermore, due to many factors, the statistics change drastically by the time those babies reach the 25-to-45 age group. Here the rate is only 95 men per 100 women, and it continues in that direction. By the time the age of 65 is reached, the figures show a scant 75 men per 100 women. The female of the species is statistically proven to be longer-lived.

At one end of the scale, medical science seeks to discover why men should be comparatively short-lived and how this trend might be altered. At the other end of the scale, where babies are concerned, efforts are being concentrated on the possibility of developing a reliable method of sex selection, so that every child may indeed be "wanted" in all senses of the word.

It is the father's sperm which actually determines whether a boy or a girl is conceived—the XX sperm produces girls, the XY sperm produces boys. These two kinds of sperm have certain differing characteristics.

A study has revealed that most men carry a greater number of the XY sperms. These are not only usually in the majority, but are also faster moving. An alkaline field favors the XY sperm. Acidity, however, can immobilize this sperm. Other points of note are its fragility and short life span. Although all factors are variable, the average XY sperm generally can retain its life-giving power for only 24 hours, or even less.

In contrast, the girl-making XX sperm is tougher, longer-lived, and slightly larger when viewed under a microscope. Also, it can survive longer in an acid environment. It also moves more slowly than its boy-making counterpart.

With these different features established, it becomes possible to aid one type of sperm while hindering the other. These are the means currently used when trying to influence conception in favor of either a boy or a girl.

METHOD 1—FOR BOYS

Since the XY sperm moves swiftly, it is likely to reach the egg waiting to be fertilized before the XX sperm. But, since its life span is short, XY must be given the optimum conditions suited to its quick pace and short life. And then, if you can give it an alkaline environment to help it along its speedy way, you'll have raised the chances of conceiving a boy.

Each human body has its individual physical and emotional quirks and the particular emotions of any given period of time can influence the physical factors. Relaxation has been termed a key to success in sex selection, because emotional tension can cause the would-be mother's body to alter its normal cycle to the point where all the careful planning is wasted.

Under normal and average circumstances, a woman is fertile for 12 to 36 hours per month. It is only at this time that the ovum is able to receive and blend with a male sperm, thus forming the nucleus of a child-to-be. This period of ovulation comes any time between the ninth and fourteenth day *after* the first day of menstruation. A menstrual cycle is usually 25 to 35 days (remember, we are talking majority averages).

To try conceiving a boy, the best method is to wait until the first few hours of ovulation are underway and then have intercourse. Abstaining for four or five days prior to this time will raise the potential father's sperm count and will also insure that no girl-producing XX sperm is anywhere near the waiting ovum. It is then advisable to abstain again (or use mechanical contraceptive methods) until the ovulation period is safely over.

To further aid the XY sperm along its way, an alkaline douche is recommended.

ALKALINE DOUCHE
1 quart warm water
2 tablespoons baking soda

Mix this solution about a half hour before intercourse is to take place. Mix slowly in a bowl, allowing the liquid to stand until the baking soda is completely dissolved. Then use in normal douche fashion, immediately before intercourse.

METHOD 2—FOR GIRLS
When a baby girl is desired, the routine is to have intercourse only up to two or three days *before* ovulation starts. The sperm will then have to wait until the would-be mother's ovum is ready—and in that waiting period the shorter-lived XY sperm will have died off. It is advisable either to abstain from intercourse during the two or three days just before ovulation, or else to use mechanical contraceptive methods.

Then, when the ovum blossoms into fertility, the patient, longer-living XX's, having made their slow way to the contact area, will be in the definite numerical majority, and the chances of a girl's being conceived increase.

An acid douche, administered before intercourse, also aids matters. It isn't only that the XX sperm prefer an acid environment, but also that such an environment can immobilize the otherwise speedy XY sperm. Thus slowed in their trajectory, the boy-making XY's are far more likely to die off before reaching the waiting ovum.

ACID DOUCHE
1 quart warm water
2 tablespoons white (malt) vinegar
Mix well together and administer immediately before intercourse.

No matter what kind of baby arrives, it's nice to know when to expect it. The following is an easy way of rapid birthdate calculation.

First take the date of the first day of the last normal menstrual period and write it down all in figures. For example, if it was June 19, you write down:

$$6 \quad 19$$

Now you add 7 to the number of days and subtract 3 from the number that denotes the month. (If you come out with a minus number in the month column, simply add 12 to it.) You then have a sum that looks like this:

$$
\begin{array}{cc}
6 & 19 \\
-3 & +7 \\
\hline
3 & 26
\end{array}
$$

The answer comes out to 3/26, which means that the baby may be expected on March 26. Remember, however, that babies have no strict sense of punctuality. You would be well advised to give the expected arrival a five-day leeway.

24.   The Mother as Environment

We all need to be ecologically aware, both of ourselves and of the earth around us. Because they are responsible for nurturing new life within them, women especially need to apply this awareness to their own bodies.

From the time of its conception until it makes its way into the world, a baby's total environment is the body of its mother. In a sense, this body has been its environment from an even earlier stage, for the ovum from which the fetus grew was formed within the mother's ovary.

Thus, for the whole prenatal stage, the child's environment is a female body: nourishment, development, and total well-being depend upon this body, from which the forming child draws its life. What the mother does or does not do can either benefit or damage the forming baby for its whole life. Under no circumstances does pollution of the physical system become so dramatic, for it is here that the consequences show up visibly in another being.

A prominent obstetrician, when asked what was the one most important thing an expectant mother could do, answered: "Keep herself as healthy as possible." This advice may at first appear to be simplistic—a fact the obstetrician himself pointed out. "That is where many mothers make their mistake," he enlarged, "they do not take into consideration the *total scope* of health."

A couple of aspirins here, a tranquilizer there. . .rather too many drinks at that marvelous party. . .heavy smoking (and coughing). . .sleeping pills on restless nights. Many pregnant women who regard themselves as healthy indulge in all the above without a twinge of conscience. As the obstetrician realized, some women do not understand the real meaning of health for themselves, in the first place—let alone have any idea of what this means in relation to their unborn child.

Naturally, the most dramatic disasters make the most dramatic headlines. The tragic lesson of thalidomide will long be remembered. But just as tragic is the mother whose too-frequent pregnancies have been responsible for her baby's abnormality. Yet there are no huge headlines about its birth. Perhaps familiarity breeds indifference. The statistics prove the point incontrovertibly: the risk of mental retardation, brain damage, and congenital malformation are all greatly increased when a woman has too many pregnancies too close together.

The main lesson to be learned from the thalidomide horror is that indiscriminate pill-taking can be disastrous. Has the lesson been taught strongly enough? The high consumption of all sorts of medications would seem to indicate otherwise. Some of these pills are no doubt necessary, but certainly not all of them. And it is quite bad enough when doctors, perhaps pestered by pregnant patients (who can't sleep or eat, feel depressed or nervous) hand out a drug prescription to dull the temporary and minor complaint—but it is that much riskier when the woman goes in for self-medication.

A drug is a drug, no matter how "mild" or "safe" it is vaunted to be, and its place is *not* within the body of a pregnant woman unless a doctor specifically says so.

There is also the danger of what is known in medical terms as drug "interaction"—the effect of one drug upon another within the human body and their joint effect upon the human system. The synergic qualities of sleeping-pills-plus-alcohol have received widespread publicity. Less known is the interactive effect of aspirin on sleeping pills, but barbiturate habitués are well-versed in boosting the effects of their pills by an aspirin or two. There are also tranquilizers which, when improperly used, have been known to promote accelerated tooth decay. Considering an unborn child's need for calcium in its forming bones, these pills would appear to be a direct threat to its healthy bone structure. The list, unfortunately, goes on and on, and at every stage the point is hammered home: indiscriminate pill-taking is the height of folly.

Let us now turn to the "social drugs"—both legal and illegal. One of the most perilous aspects of the "social drug" problem is the fact that the consequences to an unborn baby of drugs in its mother's body have not yet been fully established. But enough is known to make one thing perfectly clear: social drugs are no good for babies, in any way whatsoever.

In the extreme case of a drug such as heroin, the results are clearly seen: at birth, the infant struggles with varying degrees of violent withdrawal symptoms, and may or may not succeed in surviving the struggle. It is appalling to think of a tiny baby enduring such suffering. And who knows what psychological damage may result from this terrible experience?

The full spectrum of results from other drugs is not as clearly established. There is a theory (and research is currently being conducted on it) that a child conceived when the parents were intoxicated by alcohol has a high possibility of suffering from certain forms of mental retardation. The research, still literally at the guinea pig stage, has proved the theory correct in a high percentage of guinea pigs. Granted that guinea pigs are not people, it still gives pause for sobering thought. Enough evidence has been presented for the research to be continued.

Tobacco smoking is another thing that is known to affect the unborn child adversely. The result may be a somewhat smaller baby—or one that is stillborn. These are *known* possibilities at this stage, and research into the matter is still going on. Scientists have proved ill effects in unborn monkeys taken from tobacco-addicted mothers: damage to the blood pressure, the acid body balance, and the heart of the monkey fetuses. It is also possible that these proven prenatal problems affect the forming brain.

As to marijuana and other illegal drugs such as LSD and Methedrine—along with their legal cousins, diet pills and appetite depressants—the end results on the developing child appear to be equally harmful, although not as yet fully researched or understood. But the matter of illegality or legality is a purely secondary one: to pollute the body with *anything* that affects the developing fetus is, quite literally, a crime against nature.

A vitamin *excess* can be as damaging as a vitamin deficiency, and heaven knows, vitamin pills are legal enough. In fact, the way they are often advertised, you would think they were positively patriotic—and yet some of them, in excessive doses, can do far more harm than good, particularly if consumed by a person who has no real need for them in the first place. Gulping down vitamin pills can be as dangerous to the unborn baby as dragging in lungfuls of tobacco or marijuana smoke.

If much of the forming baby's environment is governed by the mother's good sense and knowledge, it is also true that factors in the mother's environment can adversely affect the environment she herself creates. Contagious illnesses, and those causing fever should be avoided at all costs. Although not a serious illness in itself for a normal woman, German measles can damage a fetus to the point of causing brain damage, severe eye trouble to the point of blindness, miscarriage, or stillbirth.

"The mother should keep herself as healthy as possible. . ." It now becomes obvious that the obstetricians's words cover a far wider territory than first appears. After all, if an expectant mother does not feel strongly about her own and her baby's health—why on earth is she having a baby at all? If she does not want to make any effort to give her future child the best physical and mental start possible, why give birth to it in the first place?

A child's life is what is at stake. With the advancement of sex education and most of the old sexual taboos lifted, we all know *how* babies are started. The point is, *why* do people allow them to be started, if they are not then prepared to make any effort to provide the baby not only with life, but with health as well? It would be an understatement to say that health is, after all, a baby's birthright.

Apart from the good doctor's advice on being as healthy as possible, the following pointers are of interest to those women who are planning to have a child.

As a good start, long *before* any possible pregnancy, it's an excellent idea to get the German measles threat out of the way by actually contracting the disease. I once read about a group of mothers who, on hearing a little girl in their town had contracted German measles, immediately organized a "Measle Party" to which all little girls up to the age of fourteen were invited! In any event, German measles is known as a "children's disease"—and childhood is precisely the time to get it over with, if that's possible.

A question frequently asked is when is the best age to have a baby. Ideally, the best time is when the mother is between twenty and thirty years old. This does not mean, however, that perfectly healthy babies cannot be born to older or younger women, but taking all physical and psychological factors into consideration, the decade mentioned is best.

Excellent health should be the norm right from the time of the child's conception. To conceive while ill, exhausted, drugged, or intoxicated, or even while convalescing from a serious illness, is to begin new life within a poor or a polluted environment. Medications given to a convalescent woman for an illness contracted (and basically overcome) before her pregnancy begins still affect the forming fetus. So start the health kick months ahead, and get everything off to a fresh and healthy beginning.

As far as your own environment goes, it stands to reason that the better and cleaner it is, the better your chances are of obtaining and maintaining good health. Recent studies have suggested that too high a carbon monoxide level (in, say, heavy clogged-up traffic) breathed by an expectant mother in the seventh to ninth months of her pregnancy may affect the brain development of her unborn child. The results are as yet inconclusive, but there are many similar possibilities in a congested city.

It would seem perhaps best to head for the hills or the wide open spaces during the months of pregnancy and for the actual birth. Yet there are advantages in a city (better hospital equipment, more emergency services, possibly a less physically strenuous life for the mother) that might be beneficial to both mother and child. In actual fact, it is up to each mother, guided by her physician, to decide for herself what will be best for her and her baby—if, indeed, she has a choice in the matter regarding location.

Some doctors have suggested that women who smoke should give it up three months before conceiving a child, thereby giving their bodies sufficient time to go through a natural antipollution campaign. Failing the will power to do that, they should at least cut down on their smoking drastically.

Interestingly, there are now, for the first time in a number of decades, more *non*smokers than smokers in the United States.

Even though the anti-smoking campaign has been relatively low key and low budget in comparison to the years and years of cigarette advertising, the basic message is weighty enough for people to begin to grasp. The ranks of this new majority are bound to grow, and it is to be fervently hoped that expectant mothers will join in ever-increasing numbers.

The expectant mother's health is greatly dependent on what she eats. As she feeds herself, so she feeds her child. Being an environment, she is transmitting all its life-nourishing powers and foodstuffs to the fetus developing within her. Her doctor's advice should be carefully followed, for sound medical knowledge can tailor dietary rules to the individual's particular physical needs. Never mind what Cousin Maisie had for breakfast before she had those beautiful twins: maybe her system had extra stamina and therefore could cope with peanuts-and-chocolate and two babies. Unless there is something wrong with the individual mother's physical system, her prenatal diet will be a sensibly balanced combination of nourishing foodstuffs. This is no time to go on a fad diet or give in to wild indulgences.

Both mother and unborn child need nutritive variety and sufficiency, and not only for their physical state. Recent studies have emphasized the fact that the human brain goes through its most important formative time just before and just after birth. Adequate nutrition at this time is essential to its full development, and during the prenatal stage this is achieved through the top-quality feeding of its environment, the mother.

A last, but nonetheless important reminder: the mother-to-be's state of mind and nerves reflect to some extent on the child within her. A relaxed attitude, sufficient but not excessive sleep, plenty of exercise without overtiring, and as natural and pill-free a life as possible are the best guidelines. We do not as yet understand all the links that connect our psyches to our physiological selves, but there can be no doubt that the healthy, happy mother-to-be is the best environment possible for a baby-to-be.

It would be nice if we could all become relaxed and happy

whenever we wanted, but being pregnant is not an automatic guarantee of this pleasant mental condition. A pregnant woman is vulnerable to worries and tension, the same as a nonpregnant one. However, in remembering that she is providing a total environment for an unborn child, the expectant mother can still bestow on her baby inestimable benefit, simply by exercising self-control: no self-medication, no pills or potions unless prescribed by the doctor, no fad diets, no overeating, overdrinking, or smoking.

One hopes that this is not asking too much. Let us trust that there are not too many women around who would deliberately deny a child its birthright of physical and mental normality.

25. A Reverence for Life

A child who is raised with a reverence for life will never grow up to be a despoiler of the earth.

Reverence for life means the kind of love and understanding that cherishes all living things—be they people, pets, plants, or even a tiny bug. This kind of caring needs to be developed early. The knowledge required to spark such understanding in a child is usually handed down by members of older generations. The actions of older brothers and sisters in caring for pets in the home are also influential. The importance of this early learning-to-care cannot be overestimated.

The Italians have a saying that denotes exactly the right kind of attitude: *Chi non ha cuore per le bestie, non ha cuore per i cristiani.* This translates as: "The person who does not love animals, does not love people, either."

Parents who allow (let alone encourage) their children to trample, kill, and destroy plants and animals are not only displaying their own woeful ignorance or warped mentalities, but they are also perpetuating this sort of criminally idiotic behavior. We—the human race—need this earth and all its living creatures in order to survive ourselves, and the gentle lessons that lead toward knowledge of this should begin very early indeed.

At first, these lessons are perhaps learned by behavioral osmosis—that unconscious yet constant absorption of information from one's natural surroundings. A small child who observes parents calling kindly to a dog, gently stroking a cat, chirping enthusiastically to a parakeet (who more than likely chirps right back) will soon learn to regard the living creatures around it as friends. Such a child will not suffer any unnecessary fear of animals or be terrified of a harmless passing insect.

I once had a little girl as a house guest—her first time away from her big-city home. Just before breakfast one of the first mornings she was there, I heard shrieks coming from her bedroom. As I rushed to her, I heard her screaming: "A moth! A moth!" You would have thought it was a vulture, the way she panicked. Actually, it wasn't a moth, it was a butterfly that had fluttered in on the summer warmth streaming through her window.

We spent the rest of the visit watching bugs, collecting tadpoles in a jar (and *letting them go again* after observing them at close quarters, after which we visited the pond daily, watching their gradual transformation), and generally looking at the small wildlife in the world around her.

I like to think that she returned to her own home a more knowledgeable and calmer child—at least around moths. But how many other children are brought up in this mindless hysterical way? The way that blindly stamps out life *first* and asks questions afterwards—maybe. Some never even ask.

A reverence for life is not learned overnight. After the very early years of initial observation and absorption come the years of the toddler, reaching out for experience and exploring everything at hand. It is during these years that parental guidance, supervision, and protection are *constantly essential,* and it is impossible to overemphasize this point.

The developing child, before the age of five, has not yet acquired the knowledge of certain things. His own strength, for example. Or control of his own emotions. This latter is a psychological development that comes later, as does the understanding of the difference between presence and life. Or, for that matter, departure and death.

To the small child, if an object is in his sight, it is *there* and so it is alive. If he cannot see it, it simply does not exist. Therefore, it is unreasonable for an adult to expect a small child, whose capacities are not fully developed, to understand responsibility toward another living creature, such as a household pet. The child will learn this responsibility gradually, by watching the example of the adults' behavior. But during the child's early years, the adult must teach the child by doing the tasks and demonstrating by example.

It is unreasonable, therefore, to expect young children to remember to feed the parakeet, change the dog's water regularly, give kitty a bowl of food. Children will, however, join in the doing of these tasks enthusiastically if an adult is doing them, and it is considered a privilege to be allowed to "help."

One golden rule, to protect both child's psyche and pet's life: never leave any child under five alone with a tame animal (one assumes that no one would ever leave them alone with a wild one). As I said before, knowledge of strength and control of emotion is not within the under-five's range of abilities. It is sad enough to realize that an unmeant squeeze or unintentionally rough gesture may easily kill or maim a beloved pet. Also sad—though seldom realized at the time—is the terrible damage such an experience can do to the small child's mind.

During the earliest years, choosing pets that live behind bars or glass can be an excellent form of stimulating the child's interest in animals without straining his intellectual capabilities. Goldfish, singing canaries, or cheerful colorful parakeets, are all showy to watch and can be kept safe within their enclosed environments.

After the age of five however, the normal child has undergone enough emotional development to understand the necessity for gentleness with a small pet. The responsibilities attached to having a pet should increase as the child grows older. I am reminded of the eight-year-old who, on having pleaded for a birthday present of a bunny, and having gotten her wish, was dismayed at the work involved in cleaning out the hutch (it had been established beforehand that if she got her bunny, she would keep him clean and look after him).

She grumbled about the cleaning chore in her father's hearing.

"Just be thankful it isn't a cow," he advised, briskly. The child thoughtfully went back to the cleaning job, and you could almost *see* her sense of responsibility developing! The rabbit survives to this day, healthy, much-loved, and clean.

Dogs and cats are, for the most part, the favored species for household pets. Cats housetrain quickly and easily, but puppies take somewhat longer and "puppy accidents" are all part and parcel of having a pet in the house. Since the cleaning and clearing-up responsibilities usually rest with the adults, it is worth remembering that vinegar-and-water is a quick general cleaning remedy. The thing to do is mop up the mess at once, preferably with a paper towel, and then rinse the spot with a vinegar-and-water solution. Be sure to use white vinegar.

This method, simple though it is, seems to be the best for preventing stains on carpets or lingering smells on floors. You don't have to bother much about the proportion of vinegar to water, either: just wet the paper towel under the faucet and then splash a dash of vinegar over it. Several swabs used consecutively are better than one huge one used just the once.

When an adult reacts calmly and promptly to this kind of situation, the child learns how to deal with such situations too, and he grows up with the comforting knowledge that a small puppy accident is not a tragedy (as some foolish adults would have you believe) and that there is a quick and effective method of dealing with it.

With each type of pet, individual needs are learned and different responsibilities and duties assumed. Most dogs need to be brushed. Long-haired cats need regular brushing too: short-hairs benefit from a once-or-twice a week grooming, more frequent brushing when shedding. For cats, it is a good idea to see that they have a supply of grass to chomp on, as it aids their digestion and helps prevent hairballs in their intestines during the spring when they shed. If you are an apartment dweller, this grass can be planted in pots: it is called cocks-foot grass, latin name *dactylis glomerata,* and cats love it.

Tortoises benefit from an occasional olive oil polishing of their shells. Simply saturate a wad of cotton with olive oil and rub it gently over the entire surface of their "mobile home." Canaries appreciate a sliver of apple and most birds like a cuttlefish bone on which to clean their beaks.

Water, food, and the warmth of true affection are appreciated by all pets. I've even known guinea pigs who responded visibly to human affection, and once I met a white mouse who was obviously fond of its human owner—it used to snuggle into the palm of her hand and lean against the hollow of her upcurved fingers.

Choice of pet is dependent on a number of factors: individual preference, suitability for the particular home and climatic environment, and so on. Whatever the choice, the important thing is for the child to enjoy and understand the individuality of that particular animal's life and ways; the caring for pets and the observation of nature through their particular nature are positive steps toward the learning and understanding of life in general.

Pets are not, however, the only means of acquiring this knowledge. There are many outdoor animals that do not belong to any of us in the individual sense, but are, nonetheless, all part of our lives, and are also a link in the ecological chain of life. From the city sparrow to the mountain bear, all animals should be a part of the child's growing awareness and knowledge of life.

Bird-feeding is one of the best examples of beneficial give and take between child and nature. The fun of seeing the birds come for the food encompasses both the sense of worthwhile accomplishment in helping them live and the knowledge of nature gleaned by watching them at close quarters.

According to all bird-watching and protection societies, birds will visit almost any kind of feeder, so you can either encourage youngsters to make their own feeder or buy one ready-made. The feeder's location however, is somewhat more restricted: a sunny exposure is best, one protected from the wind. If it is possible to place it near the shelter of shrubs or trees or a hedge, do so.

Bird societies also put out excellent bulletins (for free, or for a nominal amount) on how to build bird-feeders, what to feed different types of bird, which varieties to expect to see in each regional neighborhood, and so on. Since where you live will determine both which birds will attend the feeder and what form of food is best offered them, any child installing a bird-feeder should be encouraged to write away for such information. This will serve a double purpose; it will not only provide knowledge on birds, but it will also show the amount of information there is available to anyone who takes the trouble to look for it. Furthermore, it is good for a child to learn how to find and abstract the information he needs from available sources.

An important point that should be made clear to all children planning on feeding birds: once you begin feeding them, *you must continue to do so,* for they learn to rely on your feeding to sustain them. To stop suddenly in summertime is not inevitably tragic, for food is probably abundant in nature itself, and after a brief spell of hunger and confusion the birds should be able to locate other sources of nourishment. But to stop feeding birds at any point through the cold months is to risk killing them by starvation, for they have no other feeding place to turn to. Birds need time to adapt to different feeding places and habits and when they are used to finding food in one spot and then suddenly it isn't there any more, they may well starve to death before they are able to find another source.

If you find an apparently abandoned baby bird, before assuming it is an orphan make sure that there is not a nest nearby in which the bird belongs, or that a parent bird is not due to return with food supplies soon. Only when you are certain the baby bird has no one to care for it in its natural situation should you consider taking it home and looking after it yourself. Even then, there are certain precautions.

First, *handle the bird as little as possible*—these babies are very delicate creatures. Put it in a small box—a shoebox is ideal—and line the box with paper towels (these can easily be replaced for cleaning). Make sure the bird is well out of any possible draft.

Next important rule: do *not* give the baby bird any water. If you are caring for an injured adult bird, then a dish of water can be placed in a box or cage with the bird. But for babies, the rule is: NO WATER.

However, the fledgling needs food—and frequently. Very tiny

birds have to be fed every half hour: once their feathers are all grown, they can get by on hourly feeds. They should be fed until they are completely satisfied, and you'll be surprised how much it takes to satisfy a growing bird.

Birds at this stage exist mainly on protein. Most land birds need plenty of meat: they can be fed raw kidney or liver, or they will take canned dog food. Cut the meat up into small pieces—roughly ½ by 1½ inches is suitable for most fledglings. Pieces of hard-boiled eggwhite may also be given. You can use the yolk by mashing it in milk to a near-paste consistency, just wet enough to be able to roll it between the fingers. Dog biscuits soaked in milk, or raisins soaked in water and then drained, may also be given. Feed the fledgling by placing the food into its mouth with blunt tweezers or forceps. Do not push the food in or you will damage the bird's delicate throat tissue.

If you can imitate bird parents and provide some natural food as well, so much the better. Insects, worms, caterpillars, and grasshoppers are all acceptable to the fledgling, but don't give any hard-shelled insects such as beetles, as these cannot be digested.

Hopefully, the baby bird will survive: if it does, you'll have the pleasure of watching it grow at a fantastic rate (that protein diet really promotes fast growth). Then, when it is less dependent on you, it is time to think about releasing it to its natural habitat (it is against the law, incidentally, to keep a wild bird in captivity).

Work toward giving the bird its freedom gradually. Move the bird into the largest cage you can find and put the cage out into the yard or onto the porch at intervals, to enable the bird to become familiar with outdoor surroundings. Allow the bird out of its cage, for short spells to begin with, gradually increasing the length of time outside. When the bird is sufficiently developed, it will try its wings. A screened-in porch is an ideal spot for those first flying lessons.

Eventually the bird will be able to fly away, to live in natural freedom. However, this big step cannot be achieved overnight. After the bird begins to use its wings and fly away for ever-lengthening periods, it will still rely on you for food for a time, Put food out regularly and establish some kind of signal that will call the bird: a special whistle, or a bell, or just banging a spoon against a dish. Once the bird has learned how to find food for itself, it should become properly independent and then one day it will fly away altogether. You will feel sad, but you will know that by its disappearance the bird is proving that you looked after the fledgling properly and well, and restored it to its natural sphere.

Another form of flying life that you can observe at close quarters by offering it food is also one of the most beautiful and colorful forms—butterflies. These delicate insects can often be persuaded to settle and feed on a sunny windowsill if the right confection is offered them there. And confection is the right term, for butterfly food is nothing but honey and water, with a little sugar added. Half a teaspoon of honey and a half a teaspoon of sugar mixed in a cup of warm water makes an adequate butterfly nectar.

To make a feeder, you need a saucer and a wad of cotton. Butterflies, you see, taste through their feet, so you need to give them an "island" of cotton in the middle of the nectar "sea." The cotton will absorb the honey-water so that the butterfly, when it lands on the cotton will taste the food via its feet and then it will stand on the island and lower its thin rolled tongue and suck the nectar up.

A possible corollary must be faced: if there are bees and such in the garden, they may also find the nectar island. In this case, a close-up observation of bee-feeding habits may also be carried out. But children should be advised to maintain a respectful distance between themselves and the bee—preferably with a pane of glass between them if the child is a nervous one.

As a matter of fact, respect is something that should be learned in connection with *all* animals, not just those equipped with a weapon such as a sting or sharp teeth. For this, too, is part of life—to accept other forms and styles of life and life habits with respect and understanding, knowing that all creatures have their needs and their behavior patterns; and it behooves us to let them live in their way, just as we desire to live in peace in ours.

Parents who inspire their children with such knowledge of

nature are equipping them with an interest in the realities and beauties of life. Such children are unlikely to grow up to waste their time with the hollow plastic playthings of a discontented society whose members are always seeking something they can neither define nor find. For what such empty people lack is the understanding of the basic things in life. The lessons that lead toward attainment of this understanding start almost as early as life itself. Therefore parents who inspire a love of nature in their children are giving them, quite literally, the whole world.

26. Children's Gardening

Although young children seldom have the patience necessary to enjoy regular gardening, there are any number of plant- and seed-growing methods that can fascinate them. To see a bean change, step by step, from an encased blob to a plant complete with roots and stalk and leaves is an interesting project every step of the way. Watching lentils become a miniature forest is another child's delight—while carrot baskets that grow upside down are sure to amuse the younger set, too.

The advantages (from a child's point of view) of the growing methods described in this chapter are visibility and, above all, *speed*. It's all very well for an adult to plant some seed and wait the weeks or months necessary for it to germinate and start pushing shoots up. To a child, even tomorrow is a long way off. If a seed is going to take three weeks to show its growing face above the ground, you might as well forget it—the junior planter certainly will have by that time.

So for a first-time growing project, do something quick, visible, and easy. Later on, once the process of plant growth has been observed at close quarters, the gathered knowledge of what's going on beneath the soil will help the experienced junior to be patient.

Probably the best item to try the first time around is a bean-in-a-bottle. It is quick, simple, visible, and easy for a child to do and understand.

BEAN GROWING

You will need a glass jar, some blotting paper, and two or three beans, just in case one of them does not germinate. Soak the beans in water overnight before the planting.

Cut a length of blotting paper, roll it gently, and insert it into the jar. Let the roll open and widen until it lines the inside of the jar's glass surface. Insert the beans (at comfortable distances from each other) between the glass and the blotting paper, which will hold them in place. About halfway down the jar's height is a good level. Then add water to the jar; do so slowly, letting the blotting paper absorb enough moisture so that the whole surface of the paper is damp. Then add more, so that there is approximately a half inch of water in the bottom of the jar. This will insure the continued moisture of the paper.

It should be explained to the tyro gardener that the bean carries its own "growing food" within itself, so all it needs is a holding agent (the blotting paper) that transmits water to it, water being necessary to promote growth. Food and moisture being provided, its other requirement is darkness, for one is "pretending" to have planted it in the dark earth. To stimulate this darkness, the experimenter should put his bean-laden jar into a dark corner of a cupboard or a closet.

That takes care of the planting. After that, the bean jar should be "visited" once a day, for two purposes: first, to keep the water at a constant level; second, to check the growing progress—because it starts within the first few days and just keeps on going, and *fast*.

The first sign of growth will be a bump on the side of the bean (the part where it sort of folds into itself) which will soon turn into a quickly lengthening downward-growing root. From this main root, other, smaller roots will grow. Meanwhile, another bump will start appearing at the fold. This one will aim upwards; it is the shoot, eventually scheduled to turn into the stalk and put out leaves.

If instead of putting two or three beans in one jar, there are two or three jars going with one bean in each, it is easier to discover what happens when you turn a sprouted bean upside down so that its root faces up and its shoot is pointing down. (It is best to do this by gently lifting the bean away from its blotting paper surface and then reinserting it in the reversed position.) Children are usually enchanted by the results—and it shows them the tenacity of nature and demonstrates the natural rules of life and growth. For the upward-pointing root will change its direction and begin growing downward again within 24 hours, while the shoot, dismayed at finding itself in a head-down position, will also reverse its unnaturally imposed course and turn upward once more. The resulting tangle of roots and shoots as they curve back to their natural paths is far more graphic than any textbook explanation of the principle of natural growth.

As the shoot rises close to the rim of the jar, it will probably show signs of putting out a first set of leaves. This is a signal that the growing bean plant now has another requirement: light. It should therefore be brought out of the closet and placed somewhere that is light but not within the reach of direct sunlight. With light, both the shoot and its leaves will turn green, and soon a decision has to be made. If the bean plant is to continue its life, it will have to be transplanted into earth, because—as the tyro gardener will readily be able to see—all the bean nourishment has been used up in getting the plant to its present state. If it is to grow to be an "adult" bean plant, then the additional food must be provided.

If the transplanting decision is taken, either a pot or a place in a yard will do admirably. Bean plants being what they are, a pole or string should be provided, because that is what bean plants like growing up on, rather than sprawling limply along the ground.

POTATO VINES

Here is another simple-to-grow, easy-to-watch plant. The only snag is that some potato producers have a nasty habit of spraying the spuds with a chemical compound that retards or prevents sprouting. The theory is that sprouting spuds are disastrous in the kitchen and therefore to the housewife—and I suppose they are, but why keep potatoes that long, anyway? (I suspect the real beneficiary is lurking somewhere in the world of commerce and not in the ordinary kitchen.)

But if you are lucky, or buy your vegetables from a source that guarantees their organic growth, a sweet potato vine is a sure-fire success with the junior gardener. Again, a jar is needed, one with an aperture wide enough to accommodate the potato but small enough to support it. If this exact size is not available, stick three or four toothpicks around an imaginary center-circling line on the potato, and balance the spud in the mouth of the jar by resting the toothpicks on its rim. Fill the jar to the point where the bottom quarter of the potato is under water.

And there the matter rests. Direct sunshine is best avoided, but otherwise the potato vine can be grown without an initial dark-closet period. (However, the dark beginning can speed growth, so it can be worth doing it anyway, if the gardener is very young and impatient.)

The water level in the jar needs to be checked regularly, and additional water added as it is needed. Roots will grow down into the jar, and shoots will appear and climb upward; a similar decision will have to be made when the growth gets really thick for, although a potato carries more self-nourishment than a small bean, it can of course become necessary to add food for the sake of the ever-enlarging plant. However, it takes quite a while to get to that stage, and meanwhile a lot of growing greenery will have been observed and enjoyed.

CARROT CLUSTERS

Another self-feeding plant is the colorful carrot. For this gardening experiment, choose a well-developed, chubby carrot and cut it off a couple of inches from the top. This is the section you work with; the lower, thinner part can go into a stew or a salad. The fat chunk should be hollowed out on its cut end. Scoop out carefully, leaving a wall of exterior carrot all around. Then, insert a needle, threaded with thick sewing cotton, through one side of the carrot wall near the cut end and then the wall directly opposite. Tie the ends of the thread together, and you have a loop by which to hang the carrot end upside down.

Fill the scooped-out part with water and hang the carrot basket in a light place. The shoots will start sprouting out of the bottom of the basket, because that is actually the carrot's top. But, because shoots insist on growing upwards, they will naturally curve up and around, thus surrounding the carrot stump with a wall of green. Keep checking the water supply in the inner hollow; it can dry out pretty quickly in a dry atmosphere.

Another way to grow a carrot top is to slice it off about an inch thick and place it in a jar lid with water. The basket form, however, is probably the more visually attractive method—and doing both would be the most instructive.

PINEAPPLES AND TURNIPS

An odd combination, perhaps—yet these two plants also grow successfully with the sliced-top method. Place either the pineapple top or the turnip top (or both together, if you wish) into a container that holds either sand or pebbles, to keep the top in place and retain water. Leaves will sprout, their nourishment coming from the stump itself.

LENTIL FOREST

A flat dish, a paper towel or napkin, and a sprinkling of lentils is all you need here. Or, if you wish, you can substitute a layer of sand or several thicknesses of cheesecloth for the paper towel. In any event, the object is to sprinkle lentils onto a flat, moisture-retaining surface. Keep it damp, and the lentils will sprout into a green carpet within a few days.

GROWING A TREE IN A BOTTLE

Most children are fascinated by the notion of growing their very own oak tree from an acorn. The method is quite simple.

Select a few acorns from beneath a healthy-looking oak tree (since not every acorn is guaranteed to germinate). When you get the acorns home, you need a large gallon bottle with a farily narrow neck. Fill the bottle with water. Wedge the acorn in the neck of the bottle, using modeling clay to get a really secure fit.

The bottle can be kept out, but not in direct sunlight at first.

Within a short time, roots will develop down into the water and baby branches will sprout from the top of the acorn. The tree can be transferred to the garden if it thrives really well, but choose your spot carefully—remember, that's an *oak tree* you're planting!

SOIL PLANTING

All the above methods have provided moisture and a holding agent, relying on self-nourishing seeds or plant stumps to do their own feeding. The junior gardener, having seen how these things work, may well want to go onto more lasting stuff—without, however, becoming a full-fledged outdoor garden tiller. For such ambitions, the kitchen is heaven, since it will provide just about everything except the earth itself.

Cardboard egg cartons make excellent seed-starting beds; yogurt containers are another possible first-stage pot. A food can, with holes punched in the bottom for drainage, can be a full-time plant pot. And the seeds for all these are in the kitchen, too.

Fruit pits, beans, of course, onions and garlic, citrus seeds and the like are all candidates for the junior garden. And to protect the first few weeks of tender growth, there's nothing quite so good as the thin plastic bags so many groceries come in. Slip one over a pot, and you have a miniature greenhouse with a draftless atmosphere and a controlled one, too. The damp air caught inside the bag is excellent for early plant growth and removing it for normal watering won't cause any adverse effects. After watering, simply slip the bag back in place.

Not all children take to outdoor gardening simply because they have grown a bean indoors—and, indeed, why should they? But there are always those who find the steps from bean-in-paper to flowers in the soil enjoyable and challenging, and the shift from orange pits to seed packet is made with ease.

Their enthusiasm must be allowed to develop in their own individual ways and at their own paces. After all, we are hoping that the next generations will nurture the greenery of this earth because they really want to, not because they feel coerced.

27. The View Ahead

As I mentioned at the beginning of this book, we have a thirty-year period in which to clean up and shape up: a thirty-year period which is already under way. Despite the increasing amount of talk about all the pollution problems, we shall have to see a lot more action (although there is much already) in the next few years if we are to conquer the problems successfully.

Now, at this early stage of the thirty-year span, just how are things shaping up? Are people really aware and concerned? Are they cooperating and getting the job done? Is tangible progress really being achieved?

As yet, no one person can either see or give a concise report on the total picture. But there are a number of extremely encouraging signs, not only of the positive steps being taken, but also of the growing awareness and concern spreading throughout the world's population. Concerned organizations are springing up; long-established conservationist groups have taken up front-line positions—and above all, more and more people are realizing that they must listen, for their very lives are involved.

Also, in recent months, a number of triumphs have been hailed, proving that man *can* clean up the mess, and that the human mind *can* find positive solutions. For instance, there has been a statement that the means of eliminating air pollution from the automobile have been found, and it *will* be done. Cleaning systems for present engines and clean-air designs for future engines are both well beyond the experimental stage.

Specific areas have proved that waters can be cleaned up, too. Seattle, a city that began a battle against water pollution a number of years ago, is now able to point with pride to a job well done. It has taken time and effort and research money—and it has been successful. Portland is another northwestern city with a winning record in water-pollution fighting. The cleaning up of the Williamette River is not a finished task at the time of writing, but according to all reports the program is showing steady progress.

Conservation groups across the country are taking closer looks at such things as utility company contracts, resort area plans, and similar land-acquiring deals in a concentrated effort to prevent further ravaging of forest lands and wilderness areas so vital to the balance of plant and animal life.

On a more personal level, women who wear fur coats made of skins of endangered species are being made to feel more and more uncomfortable. "I keep getting cold stares," an acquaintance confessed to me a few days ago, "and yesterday a woman came up to me on the street and scolded me right there, in front of all the passersby!" That woman's courage has had the desired effect, for I doubt very much that my friend's leopard-skin coat is going to be worn much more. People *do* care what others say about them—eecially in public.

Another personal stance being taken is one that concerns men. Men as well as women are becoming more and more aware of the population explosion and its threats of danger, and they appear to be willing to take definite steps to prevent overpopulation. The number of vasectomies performed in the United States has almost trebled in the last two years, and it is estimated that within the next year, half a million men in the United States will undergo the twenty-minute operation that allows them to enjoy their virility without further recourse to contraceptive procedures.

Both the United States and the U.S.S.R. are working on technological programs with the view to launching ecology-guard satellites within the next few years. These are expected to perform such helpful tasks as detecting thermal and chemical pollution, alerting forest agencies on forest fires, measuring humidity rates and changing currents, both in the air and in the oceans, and generally acting as early-bird guardians over all natural spheres.

While governments work on vast projects, people work on smaller, but equally important ones, for each link in the chain has its purpose and must maintain its strength. A mechanized scarecrow has recently been patented. This contribution may well be a partial solution to the problem of poisons in our food. To scare birds away from a bed of vegetables by means of an animated scarecrow seems far safer, in the long run, than spraying the area with some noxious form of bird repellent that may soak into the vegetables and thus find its way into human stomachs.

A similar invention, also recently patented, is said to achieve the same end by using noise instead of motion. This may prove effective against a wide range of pests, since the sound is beyond the range of human hearing (rather like a dog whistle) and bothersome and therefore frightening to a number of creatures, without disturbing the atmosphere for people. It is, in effect, a contemporary version of the old-time "beaters," who in certain countries would go into the fields armed with metal noise-making objects and clang them ceaselessly to frighten the current pest away.

Elsewhere the battle is being fought on many different levels. Governments, organizations, and even individuals are getting more involved in ecological campaigns. Canada was one of the first countries to blow the whistle on phosphates: Russia has placed the polar bear under protection (and it's about time that Alaska did, too). Solid waste is being dried and used to fuel power stations in Essen, Germany, while the insect-control virtues of the shy and harmless hedgehog are being well advertised in the United Kingdom.

I could cite countless other instances to show that the situation is encouraging. People are becoming increasingly aware: they are doing things to help solve the problems and they are prodding industry and government into action, as well.

There are bad spots, too, no two ways about it.

Stubbornness and ignorance and pigheadedness and self-interest—ecological improvement is held back by the suicidally selfish attitude of those who think that if they can get what they want, the rest of the world doesn't matter. Such attitudes, however, are not only morally wrong, they are totally out of date, for the time when one could get away with that sort of thinking went out with the beginning of the thirty-year span. It is no longer a question of one *should* not think or act in that way; one *cannot* do so any more, for time is no longer on our side.

The eutrophication of Lake Erie dramatically demonstrates this fact. The mounting evidence on mercury, lead, and other metals in foodstuffs is another. The possible danger of eating certain game birds, because of the insecticide content of their bodies is yet another form of proof that heedless action can backfire.

Of course, there are diehards. They crop up in all sorts of places—television, neighborhood committees—and sometimes even right next door. On a person-to-person level the ecologically aware individual can often do a gentle job of convincing his recalcitrant neighbor: further up the scale, it takes a bit more doing.

Nonetheless, it is possible. Under the headline, DETERGENT SPOKESMEN DENY NEED FOR WIDENING BAN appeared an indignant protest, but government officials decided that the ban was indeed going to go into effect in other areas. These officials did not reach this decision by a form of interior spontaneous combustion: their opinion was formed by the concentrated efforts of numbers of concerned citizens, some of them scientists, some of them housewives, all of them fed up with suds coming out of their faucets. There are times when you don't have to be an expert to realize that something is wrong.

The technology boys thinking up new disposables should be encouraged—maybe *firmly*—to channel their technological talents to sounder use. Granted that some things should be disposable—I have already mentioned examples in an earlier chapter—the thought of more and more disposables being developed is a dreadful one. Fortunately, there are those among the ranks of the engineers who are beginning to point out the snags in disposing of disposables.

An area thick with diehards is the border where business and politics meet. POLLUTERS SIT ON ANTIPOLLUTION BOARDS was the headline on a recent newspaper story, and the facts and figures quoted were grim. Government antipollution boards are set up, presumably in good faith, and then industrialists, whose factories poison rivers and belch foul smoke into the air, quickly rush to join the committees. There, while mouthing pious platitudes, they do their best to protect their own interests. For them, the pollution always comes from the other guy's factory— the guy who didn't get onto the antipollution board. But in the long run this sort of thing isn't going to work. After all, people have been alerted by the newspapers—and knowing what the problem is can be half the battle in solving it.

Another bunch of diehards can be found figuratively wrapped in

plastic. RECYCLING OF PLASTICS HELD 10 YEARS AWAY
was the head on a recent report, and the plastics people solemnly
stated that incineration was the *only* way of dealing with their
product after it had served its primary—and at present, only—use.
But people might just decide that another way is to use a lot less
of the product. And when they do, the plastics industry will
"suddenly" discover a way to reuse or safely dispose of the
products they make. The trouble with incinerating much of it is
that it pours particularly harmful material into the air; this is
already scientifically established. If people push the manufacturers
by cutting down their plastic purchases, the manufacturers are
going to find ecologically sound methods of rechanneling or
recycling or disposing of their product.

Cries of "unfair to industry" or "ruining business" will not raise
much sympathy. Times change, and so do needs. What was
commercially viable ten years ago is not necessarily so today.
Industry and commerce, just like people and life, must change
with the times. After all, the rack-makers in the Middle Ages
probably believed their industry would go on forever, what with
the Inquisition being such a steady customer.

In the first section of the thirty-year cleanup span there is going
to be a certain amount of push-me-pull-you in all sectors as
opposed factions clash, as the ecologically aware meet the diehards
head on.

For instance, let's look at the world of investment. The
following is directly quoted from a recent investment news
bulletin:

> Prospects for glass container activities are especially bright.
> The growth momentum in usage of one-way bottles is expected
> to continue. . . .

Investment people tend to talk in overripe terms like that; what
they mean is they expect the throwaway bottle to be Big Business
in the future. So step right this way, folks, put your money on the
no-deposit, no-return bottle.

Except that I wouldn't, if I were you. Because in other parts of the industry, more forward-looking views are being taken. One soft-drink company has already upped the bottle-deposit sum, to encourage the return of bottles. More companies are going to follow. The nonreturnable bottle is going to get an increasingly unfavorable reputation (as it should). The business of recycling bottles is already on the upswing. Perhaps the government would even step in and declare no-return bottles unlawful.

And just where are those investor-bulletin writers going to be then? Actually, I think I know. Either they will be harrumphing into their newspapers, complaining that the world isn't what it used to be, or they'll have switched attitudes and joined the winners, and be busily promoting a company that recycles bottles. And the fact of the matter is that the new attitudes *will* eventually pay.

Industry and commerce being part of our civilization, there is nothing to be gained by running either into the ground. There are goods and products we need: it is the means of making and distributing them that will, in certain cases, have to be changed.

Watchdog agencies will have to sort out the doers from the mere claimers and see to it that progress is kept up continually. For textile mills to say they have "virtually eliminated water pollution" in their area is a marvelous claim; now let's make sure that the achievement matches up to the press release. The claims of the gasoline companies and the chemical companies will similarly have to be followed up.

As I come to the end of this book, I should like to emphasize that the subject itself is neither closed nor ended. Nor has the last word been written, for there are always more things and new ways to discover, to be told, to work out for oneself, that will help us live our lives in the best, healthiest, and most natural ways, while enabling the earth itself to be healthy and naturally replenishing.

You will find that if you are aware of the problem (and you must be, if you have read this far), you will be tuned in to the changes that will be occurring from day to day. Since you will be keeping this automatic watch, take advantage of the items that it leads you to discover, and get your friends to do the same. There will be more and more recycling programs initiated, many of them at the community level. Bottles and aluminum are already being returned to bottlers and aluminum manufacturers, with the money incentive paving the way, and other industries will follow suit.

Because if we don't care, who will? This is our earth, our world: the idea of a clean and healthy place to live is not a fad, it's a fact of life.

Since ecology is a subject as serious and vital as life itself, I can think of no better way to close this book than by quoting The Epistle of Paul the Apostle to the Philippians, Chapter IV, verse 8:

Finally, brethren, whatsoever things are true, whatsoever things are honest, whatsoever things are just, whatsoever things are pure, whatsoever things are lovely, whatsoever things are of good report; if there be any virtue, and if there be any praise, think on these things.

Some Ecologically Minded Agencies

Environmental Action
1346 Connecticut Avenue, N.W., Room 731, Washington, D.C. 20036

Friends of the Earth
30 East 42nd Street, New York, N.Y. 10017

World Wildlife Fund
910 Seventeenth Street, N.W., Room 619, Washington, D.C. 20006

National Audubon Society
1130 Fifth Avenue, New York, N.Y. 10028

National Wildlife Federation
1412 Sixteenth Street, N.W., Washington, D.C. 20036

Sierra Club
1050 Mills Tower, San Francisco, Calif. 94104

To form your own consumer-oriented organization, write for a free manual to:
The President's Committee on Consumer Interests, Washington, D.C. 20506

INDEX